RESURRECTING
REAGAN

RESURRECTING
REAGAN

JUDGE HAL MOROZ

NEW YORK   ATLANTA   WASHINGTON

Resurrecting Reagan

Judge Hal Moroz

Copyright © 2014 by Harold Ronald Moroz

Access to the public addresses and statements of our 40th President of the United States is available through a wide range of sources in the public domain.
The author of this work wishes to acknowledge the exceptionally outstanding archives of The Ronald Reagan Presidential Foundation located in Simi Valley, California.
The author is a member of the Foundation, and encourages everyone interested in supporting and preserving the legacy of President Ronald Reagan to join the Foundation. Membership can be obtained by writing The Ronald Reagan Presidential Foundation, 40 Presidential Drive, Simi Valley, California 93065, or via the internet at www.reaganfoundation.org.

Unless otherwise noted, Scripture quotations are from
The King James Version of the Bible.

Printed in the United States of America

"I do not believe in a fate that will fall on us no matter what we do. I do believe in a fate that will fall on us if we do nothing. So, with all the creative energy at our command, let us begin an era of national renewal. Let us renew our determination, our courage, and our strength. And let us renew our faith and our hope.

"We have every right to dream heroic dreams. Those who say that we are in a time when there are no heroes just don't know where to look. You can see heroes every day going in and out of factory gates. Others, a handful in number, produce enough food to feed all of us and then the world beyond. You meet heroes across a counter -- and they are on both sides of that counter. There are entrepreneurs with faith in themselves and faith in an idea who create new jobs, new wealth and opportunity. They are individuals and families whose taxes support the government and whose voluntary gifts support church, charity, culture, art, and education. Their patriotism is quiet but deep. Their values sustain our national life.

"I have used the words 'they' and 'their' in speaking of these heroes. I could say 'you' and 'your' because I am addressing the heroes of whom I speak -- you, the citizens of this blessed land. Your dreams, your hopes, your goals are going to be the dreams, the hopes, and the goals of this administration, so help me God."

~ President Ronald Reagan
Inaugural Address, January 20, 1981

Resurrecting Reagan

Contents

Introduction

The Age of Reagan

"But I never thought it was my style or the words I used that made a difference: it was the content. I wasn't a great communicator, but I communicated great things, and they didn't spring full bloom from my brow, they came from the heart of a great nation--from our experience, our wisdom, and our belief in the principles that have guided us for two centuries. They called it the Reagan Revolution. Well, I'll accept that, but for me it always seemed more like The Great Re-Discovery, a re-discovery of our values and our common sense."

~ President Ronald Reagan
Farewell Address, January 11, 1989

President Ronald Reagan was a Great Communicator, but first and foremost he was a Great American. He was a man of faith, with a vision for our country, gifted with the ability to powerfully communicate his ideas. His patriotism resonated throughout our country. And it was his genuine love of America that fueled his resolve to bring our country back from the brink. Quite simply, he inspired the best in us!

I first met Governor Ronald Reagan in 1980. He was on the campaign trail with Congressman Jack Kemp in Queens, New York. He was seeking the presidency, and I was a graduate student at St. John's University. Governor Reagan was my hero, because he loved America and worked tirelessly to improve her, and he embodied the vision and ideals that made America great. He believed in American Exceptionalism --- and he made us believe in it too! But when I first met him, and shook his hand, America was in decline. The liberal politicians lost the War in Vietnam, Jimmy Carter was our impotent president, and the torch of liberty had not so dimmed in our two-hundred-plus years of history. We were on a precipice. As candidate Ronald Reagan said on that fateful day,

"You and I have a rendezvous with destiny.
We will preserve for our children this,
the last best hope of man on earth,
or we will sentence them to take the first step
into a thousand years of darkness.
If we fail, at least let our children and our children's children
say of us we justified our brief moment here.
We did all that could be done."

It was a pivotal moment in the history of our republic. And later that year, Ronald Reagan was elected the 40th President of the United States, and America began her march down the long road to recovery. His campaign slogan was "Let's Make America Great Again!" I accepted it as his pledge to lead a national crusade to bring America back from the brink. Praise God, President Reagan kept that pledge!

President Ronald Reagan was the right man, at the right time, to lead America back to greatness! And this book is a tribute to this great, good man!

President Reagan was a great believer in God and country! On more than one occasion, he declared, "I believe that God put this land between two great oceans to be found by a special people from every corner of the world who had that extra love of freedom that prompted them to leave their homeland and come to this land to make it a brilliant light beam of freedom to the world." His leadership and faith made me a believer and crusader in the cause.

I continue to herald the virtues of President Reagan, even to the present day. He was a great leader and visionary! And he taught us much about America, and the leadership it needs to survive and prosper. He brought America back, and in the process changed many lives, including mine. He became president less than a month before his 70th birthday, and changed my perspective on age. President Reagan was a favorite and champion of both the young and old. So much so, he was often mocked and trivialized by the liberal media pundits, but he soundly defeated Jimmy Carter and changed the political landscape of the South. And that same liberal media questioned his conservative agenda for America, but he restored our economy and our respect around the world, and managed to win re-election by a landslide, achieving victory in 49 of the 50 states in our Union, and coming very close to winning the home state of his democrat opponent. President Reagan gave no quarter to his opponents, defeating them in their liberal strongholds. He surrendered no states in the electoral process. All were contested and in play. He made an end to abortion, reduced taxes, and national defense Republican issues. He rebuilt our military and restored the great American Spirit. President Reagan made me realize that with God all things are possible.

Within this work are the philosophy and body of evidence -- the blueprint, if you will -- to recapture and sustain America's march to greatness. Ronald Reagan's key speeches are documented in this book, a priceless collection of selected thoughts and utterances of a man who changed the course of American history, and laid the foundation to restore America's greatness, making us truly the last best hope of man on earth. This is his legacy, one worth resurrecting and studying by this generation, and the generations of Americans to come.

Beginning with the start of a national crusade in his inaugural address, and culminating in his passing the torch to us with his powerful farewell, President Reagan points the way to building a better America. What then follows is a retracement of his political journey through his many moving speeches and statements. And finally, you will find a tribute to the man, and a challenge to continue the legacy of the greatest president of our lifetime.

Much damage has been done in the decades since he concluded his service at President and Commander-in-Chief, especially by the likes of Bill Clinton and Barack Hussein Obama, but the legacy of President Ronald Reagan lives on! And it lives on in "We the People," citizens like you and me who were inspired by the great words and good deeds of President Reagan. We participated in the "Reagan Revolution," and it is now up to us to carry the banner of conservative principles that he championed to this generation and the next. We must stand in the gap for America!

And you can start this quest by reading passages from this book to your family around the dinner table – and why not start this tradition tonight? Study it, and live it! Now that would be a very American thing to do!

With God's help, and your contributions to this noble effort, we can fulfill President Reagan's vision that "America's best days are yet to come!" Let us pray this is so! "And, after all," as President Reagan observed in his first inaugural address, "why shouldn't we believe that? We are Americans!" This is the Age of Reagan! Let's Resurrect his memory, and ...

"Let's Make America Great Again!"

~ Judge Hal Moroz

~ * ~

"We need you. We need your youth. We need your strength. We need your idealism to help us make right that which is wrong. Each generation goes further than the generation preceding it because it stands on the shoulders of that generation. You will have opportunities beyond anything we've ever known."

~ President Ronald Reagan, May 17, 1981

Hail & Farewell

President Reagan's First Inaugural Address

January 20, 1981

Senator Hatfield, Mr. Chief Justice, Mr. President, Vice President Bush, Vice President Mondale, Senator Baker, Speaker O'Neill, Reverend Moomaw, and my fellow citizens: To a few of us here today, this is a solemn and most momentous occasion; and yet, in the history of our nation, it is a commonplace occurrence. The orderly transfer of authority as called for in the Constitution routinely takes place as it has for almost two centuries and few of us stop to think how unique we really are. In the eyes of many in the world, this every-4-year ceremony we accept as normal is nothing less than a miracle.

Mr. President, I want our fellow citizens to know how much you did to carry on this tradition. By your gracious cooperation in the transition process, you have shown a watching world that we are a united people pledged to maintaining a political system which guarantees individual liberty to a greater degree than any other, and I thank you and your people for all your help in maintaining the continuity which is the bulwark of our Republic.

The business of our nation goes forward. These United States are confronted with an economic affliction of great proportions. We suffer from the longest and one of the worst sustained inflations in our national history. It distorts our economic decisions, penalizes thrift, and crushes the struggling young and the fixed-income elderly alike. It threatens to shatter the lives of millions of our people.

Idle industries have cast workers into unemployment, causing human misery and personal indignity. Those who do work are denied a fair return for their labor by a tax system which penalizes successful achievement and keeps us from maintaining full productivity.

But great as our tax burden is, it has not kept pace with public spending. For decades, we have piled deficit upon deficit, mortgaging our future and our children's future for the temporary convenience of the present. To continue this long trend is to guarantee tremendous social, cultural, political, and economic upheavals.

You and I, as individuals, can, by borrowing, live beyond our means, but for only a limited period of time. Why, then, should we think that collectively, as a nation, we are not bound by that same limitation?

We must act today in order to preserve tomorrow. And let there be no misunderstanding--we are going to begin to act, beginning today.

The economic ills we suffer have come upon us over several decades. They will not go away in days, weeks, or months, but they will go away. They will go away because we, as Americans, have the capacity now, as we have had in the past, to do whatever needs to be done to preserve this last and greatest bastion of freedom.

In this present crisis, government is not the solution to our problem.

From time to time, we have been tempted to believe that society has become too complex to be managed by self-rule, that government by an elite group is superior to government for, by, and of the people. But if no one among us is capable of governing himself, then who among us has the capacity to govern someone else? All of us together, in and out of government, must bear the burden. The solutions we seek must be equitable, with no one group singled out to pay a higher price.

We hear much of special interest groups. Our concern must be for a special interest group that has been too long neglected. It knows no sectional boundaries or ethnic and racial divisions, and it crosses political party lines. It is made up of men and women who raise our food, patrol our streets, man our mines and our factories, teach our children, keep our homes, and heal us when we are sick-- professionals, industrialists, shopkeepers, clerks, cabbies, and truck drivers. They are, in short, "We the people," this breed called Americans.

Well, this administration's objective will be a healthy, vigorous, growing economy that provides equal opportunity for all Americans, with no barriers born of bigotry or discrimination. Putting America back to work means putting all Americans back to work. Ending inflation means freeing all Americans from the terror of runaway living costs. All must share in the productive work of this "new beginning" and all must share in the bounty of a revived economy. With the idealism and fair play which are the core of our system and our strength, we can have a strong and prosperous America at peace with itself and the world.

So, as we begin, let us take inventory. We are a nation that has a government--not the other way around. And this makes us special among the nations of the Earth. Our government has no power except that granted it by the people. It is time to check and reverse the growth of government which shows signs of having grown beyond the consent of the governed.

It is my intention to curb the size and influence of the Federal establishment and to demand recognition of the distinction between the powers granted to the Federal Government and those reserved to the States or to the people. All of us need to be reminded that the Federal Government did not create the States; the States created the Federal Government.

Now, so there will be no misunderstanding, it is not my intention to do away with government. It is, rather, to make it work--work with us, not over us; to stand by our side, not ride on our back. Government can and must provide opportunity, not smother it; foster productivity, not stifle it.

If we look to the answer as to why, for so many years, we achieved so much, prospered as no other people on Earth, it was because here, in this land, we unleashed the energy and individual genius of man to a greater extent than has ever been done before. Freedom and the dignity of the individual have been more available and assured here than in any other place on Earth. The price for this freedom at times has been high, but we have never been unwilling to pay that price.

It is no coincidence that our present troubles parallel and are proportionate to the intervention and intrusion in our lives that result from unnecessary and excessive growth of government. It is time for us to realize that we are too great a nation to limit ourselves to small dreams. We are not, as some would have us believe, doomed to an inevitable decline. I do not believe in a fate that will fall on us no matter what we do. I do believe in a fate that will fall on us if we do nothing. So, with all the creative energy at our command, let us begin an era of national renewal. Let us renew our determination, our courage, and our strength. And let us renew our faith and our hope.

We have every right to dream heroic dreams. Those who say that we are in a time when there are no heroes just don't know where to look. You can see heroes every day going in and out of factory gates. Others, a handful in number, produce enough food to feed all of us and then the world beyond. You meet heroes across a counter--and they are on both sides of that counter. There are entrepreneurs with faith in themselves and faith in an idea who create new jobs, new wealth and opportunity. They are individuals and families whose taxes support the government and whose voluntary gifts support church, charity, culture, art, and education. Their patriotism is quiet but deep. Their values sustain our national life.

I have used the words "they" and "their" in speaking of these heroes. I could say "you" and "your" because I am addressing the heroes of whom I speak--you, the citizens of this blessed land. Your dreams, your hopes, your goals are going to be the dreams, the hopes, and the goals of this administration, so help me God.

We shall reflect the compassion that is so much a part of your makeup. How can we love our country and not love our countrymen, and loving them, reach out a hand when they fall, heal them when they are sick, and provide opportunities to make them self-sufficient so they will be equal in fact and not just in theory?

Can we solve the problems confronting us? Well, the answer is an unequivocal and emphatic "yes." To paraphrase Winston Churchill, I did not take the oath I have just taken with the intention of presiding over the dissolution of the world's strongest economy.

In the days ahead I will propose removing the roadblocks that have slowed our economy and reduced productivity. Steps will be taken aimed at restoring the balance between the various levels of government. Progress may be slow--measured in inches and feet, not miles--but we will progress. It is time to reawaken this industrial giant, to get government back within its means, and to lighten our punitive tax burden. And these will be our first priorities, and on these principles, there will be no compromise.

On the eve of our struggle for independence a man who might have been one of the greatest among the Founding Fathers, Dr. Joseph Warren, President of the Massachusetts Congress, said to his fellow Americans, "Our country is in danger, but not to be despaired of.... On you depend the fortunes of America. You are to decide the important questions upon which rests the happiness and the liberty of millions yet unborn. Act worthy of yourselves."

Well, I believe we, the Americans of today, are ready to act worthy of ourselves, ready to do what must be done to ensure happiness and liberty for ourselves, our children and our children's children.

And as we renew ourselves here in our own land, we will be seen as having greater strength throughout the world. We will again be the exemplar of freedom and a beacon of hope for those who do not now have freedom.

To those neighbors and allies who share our freedom, we will strengthen our historic ties and assure them of our support and firm commitment. We will match loyalty with loyalty. We will strive for mutually beneficial relations. We will not use our friendship to impose on their sovereignty, for our own sovereignty is not for sale.

As for the enemies of freedom, those who are potential adversaries, they will be reminded that peace is the highest aspiration of the American people. We will negotiate for it, sacrifice for it; we will not surrender for it--now or ever.

Our forbearance should never be misunderstood. Our reluctance for conflict should not be misjudged as a failure of will. When action is required to preserve our national security, we will act. We will maintain sufficient strength to prevail if need be, knowing that if we do so we have the best chance of never having to use that strength.

Above all, we must realize that no arsenal, or no weapon in the arsenals of the world, is so formidable as the will and moral courage of free men and women. It is a weapon our adversaries in today's world do not have. It is a weapon that we as Americans do have. Let that be understood by those who practice terrorism and prey upon their neighbors.

I am told that tens of thousands of prayer meetings are being held on this day, and for that I am deeply grateful. We are a nation under God, and I believe God intended for us to be free. It would be fitting and good, I think, if on each Inauguration Day in future years it should be declared a day of prayer.

This is the first time in history that this ceremony has been held, as you have been told, on this West Front of the Capitol. Standing here, one faces a magnificent vista, opening up on this city's special beauty and history. At the end of this open mall are those shrines to the giants on whose shoulders we stand.

Directly in front of me, the monument to a monumental man: George Washington, father of our country. A man of humility who came to greatness reluctantly. He led America out of revolutionary victory into infant nationhood. Off to one side, the stately memorial to Thomas Jefferson. The Declaration of Independence flames with his eloquence.

And then beyond the Reflecting Pool the dignified columns of the Lincoln Memorial. Whoever would understand in his heart the meaning of America will find it in the life of Abraham Lincoln.

Beyond those monuments to heroism is the Potomac River, and on the far shore the sloping hills of Arlington National Cemetery with its row on row of simple white markers bearing crosses or Stars of David. They add up to only a tiny fraction of the price that has been paid for our freedom.

Each one of those markers is a monument to the kinds of hero I spoke of earlier. Their lives ended in places called Belleau Wood, The Argonne, Omaha Beach, Salerno and halfway around the world on Guadalcanal, Tarawa, Pork Chop Hill, the Chosin Reservoir, and in a hundred rice paddies and jungles of a place called Vietnam.

Under one such marker lies a young man--Martin Treptow--who left his job in a small town barbershop in 1917 to go to France with the famed Rainbow Division. There, on the western front, he was killed trying to carry a message between battalions under heavy artillery fire.

We are told that on his body was found a diary. On the flyleaf under the heading, "My Pledge," he had written these words: "America must win this war. Therefore, I will work, I will save, I will sacrifice, I will endure, I will fight cheerfully and do my utmost, as if the issue of the whole struggle depended on me alone."

The crisis we are facing today does not require of us the kind of sacrifice that Martin Treptow and so many thousands of others were called upon to make. It does require, however, our best effort, and our willingness to believe in ourselves and to believe in our capacity to perform great deeds; to believe that together, with God's help, we can and will resolve the problems which now confront us.

And, after all, why shouldn't we believe that? We are Americans! God bless you, and thank you.

President Reagan's Farewell Speech

January 11, 1989

This is the 34th time I'll speak to you from the Oval Office and the last. We've been together 8 years now, and soon it'll be time for me to go. But before I do, I wanted to share some thoughts, some of which I've been saving for a long time.

It's been the honor of my life to be your President. So many of you have written the past few weeks to say thanks, but I could say as much to you. Nancy and I are grateful for the opportunity you gave us to serve.

One of the things about the Presidency is that you're always somewhat apart. You spent a lot of time going by too fast in a car someone else is driving, and seeing the people through tinted glass--the parents holding up a child, and the wave you saw too late and couldn't return. And so many times I wanted to stop and reach out from behind the glass, and connect. Well, maybe I can do a little of that tonight.

People ask how I feel about leaving. And the fact is, "parting is such sweet sorrow." The sweet part is California and the ranch and freedom. The sorrow--the goodbyes, of course, and leaving this beautiful place.

You know, down the hall and up the stairs from this office is the part of the White House where the President and his family live. There are a few favorite windows I have up there that I like to stand and look out of early in the morning. The view is over the grounds here to the Washington Monument, and then the Mall and the

Jefferson Memorial. But on mornings when the humidity is low, you can see past the Jefferson to the river, the Potomac, and the Virginia shore. Someone said that's the view Lincoln had when he saw the smoke rising from the Battle of Bull Run. I see more prosaic things: the grass on the banks, the morning traffic as people make their way to work, now and then a sailboat on the river.

I've been thinking a bit at that window. I've been reflecting on what the past 8 years have meant and mean. And the image that comes to mind like a refrain is a nautical one--a small story about a big ship, and a refugee, and a sailor. It was back in the early eighties, at the height of the boat people. And the sailor was hard at work on the carrier Midway, which was patrolling the South China Sea. The sailor, like most American servicemen, was young, smart, and fiercely observant. The crew spied on the horizon a leaky little boat. And crammed inside were refugees from Indochina hoping to get to America. The Midway sent a small launch to bring them to the ship and safety. As the refugees made their way through the choppy seas, one spied the sailor on deck, and stood up, and called out to him. He yelled, "Hello, American sailor. Hello, freedom man."

A small moment with a big meaning, a moment the sailor, who wrote it in a letter, couldn't get out of his mind. And, when I saw it, neither could I. Because that's what it was to be an American in the 1980's. We stood, again, for freedom. I know we always have, but in the past few years the world again--and in a way, we ourselves--rediscovered it.

It's been quite a journey this decade, and we held together through some stormy seas. And at the end, together, we are reaching our destination.

The fact is, from Grenada to the Washington and Moscow summits, from the recession of '81 to '82, to the expansion that began in late '82 and continues to this day, we've made a difference. The way I see it, there were two great triumphs, two things that I'm proudest of. One is the economic recovery, in which the people of America created--and filled--19 million new jobs. The other is the recovery of our morale. America is respected again in the world and looked to for leadership.

Something that happened to me a few years ago reflects some of this. It was back in 1981, and I was attending my first big economic summit, which was held that year in Canada. The meeting place rotates among the member countries. The opening meeting was a formal dinner of the heads of government of the seven industrialized nations. Now, I sat there like the new kid in school and listened, and it was all Francois this and Helmut that. They dropped titles and spoke to one another on a first-name basis. Well, at one point I sort of leaned in and said, "My name's Ron." Well, in that same year, we began the actions we felt would ignite an economic comeback--cut taxes and regulation, started to cut spending. And soon the recovery began.

Two years later, another economic summit with pretty much the same cast. At the big opening meeting we all got together, and all of a sudden, just for a moment, I saw that everyone was just sitting there looking at me. And then one of them broke the silence. "Tell us about the American miracle," he said.

Well, back in 1980, when I was running for President, it was all so different. Some pundits said our programs would result in catastrophe. Our views on foreign affairs would cause war. Our plans for the economy would cause inflation to soar and bring about economic collapse. I even remember one highly respected economist saying, back in 1982, that "The engines of economic growth have shut down here, and they're likely to stay that way for years to come." Well, he and the other opinion leaders were wrong. The fact is what they call "radical" was really "right." What they called "dangerous" was just "desperately needed."

And in all of that time I won a nickname, "The Great Communicator." But I never thought it was my style or the words I used that made a difference: it was the content. I wasn't a great communicator, but I communicated great things, and they didn't spring full bloom from my brow, they came from the heart of a great nation--from our experience, our wisdom, and our belief in the principles that have guided us for two centuries. They called it the Reagan revolution. Well, I'll accept that, but for me it always seemed more like the great rediscovery, a rediscovery of our values and our common sense.

Common sense told us that when you put a big tax on something, the people will produce less of it. So, we cut the people's tax rates, and the people produced more than ever before. The economy bloomed like a plant that had been cut back and could now grow quicker and stronger. Our economic program brought about the longest peacetime expansion in our history: real family income up, the poverty rate down, entrepreneurship booming, and an explosion in research and new technology. We're exporting more than ever because American industry became more competitive, and at the same time, we summoned the national will to knock down protectionist walls abroad instead of erecting them at home.

Common sense also told us that to preserve the peace, we'd have to become strong again after years of weakness and confusion. So, we rebuilt our defenses, and this New Year we toasted the new peacefulness around the globe. Not only have the superpowers actually begun to reduce their stockpiles of nuclear weapons--and hope for even more progress is bright--but the regional conflicts that rack the globe are also beginning to cease. The Persian Gulf is no longer a war zone. The Soviets are leaving Afghanistan. The Vietnamese are preparing to pull out of Cambodia, and an American-mediated accord will soon send 50,000 Cuban troops home from Angola.

The lesson of all this was, of course, that because we're a great nation, our challenges seem complex. It will always be this way. But as long as we remember our first principles and believe in ourselves, the future will always be ours. And something else we learned: Once you begin a great movement, there's no telling where it will end. We meant to change a nation, and instead, we changed a world.

Countries across the globe are turning to free markets and free speech and turning away from the ideologies of the past. For them, the great rediscovery of the 1980's has been that, lo and behold, the moral way of government is the practical way of government: Democracy, the profoundly good, is also the profoundly productive.

When you've got to the point when you can celebrate the anniversaries of your 39th birthday, you can sit back sometimes, review your life, and see it flowing before you. For me there was a fork in the river, and it was right in the middle of my life. I never meant to go into politics. It wasn't my intention when I was young.

But I was raised to believe you had to pay your way for the blessings bestowed on you. I was happy with my career in the entertainment world, but I ultimately went into politics because I wanted to protect something precious.

Ours was the first revolution in the history of mankind that truly reversed the course of government, and with three little words: "We the People." "We the People" tell the government what to do; it doesn't tell us. "We the People" are the driver; the government is the car. And we decide where it should go, and by what route, and how fast. Almost all the world's constitutions are documents in which governments tell the people what their privileges are. Our Constitution is a document in which "We the People" tell the government what it is allowed to do. "We the People" are free. This belief has been the underlying basis for everything I've tried to do these past 8 years.

But back in the 1960's, when I began, it seemed to me that we'd begun reversing the order of things--that through more and more rules and regulations and confiscatory taxes, the government was taking more of our money, more of our options, and more of our freedom. I went into politics in part to put up my hand and say, "Stop." I was a citizen politician, and it seemed the right thing for a citizen to do.

I think we have stopped a lot of what needed stopping. And I hope we have once again reminded people that man is not free unless government is limited. There's a clear cause and effect here that is as neat and predictable as a law of physics: As government expands, liberty contracts.

Nothing is less free than pure communism--and yet we have, the past few years, forged a satisfying new closeness with the Soviet Union. I've been asked if this isn't a gamble, and my answer is no, because we're basing our actions not on words but deeds. The detente of the 1970's was based not on actions but promises. They'd promise to treat their own people and the people of the world better. But the gulag was still the gulag, and the state was still expansionist, and they still waged proxy wars in Africa, Asia, and Latin America.

Well, this time, so far, it's different. President Gorbachev has brought about some internal democratic reforms and begun the withdrawal from Afghanistan. He has also freed prisoners whose names I've given him every time we've met.

But life has a way of reminding you of big things through small incidents. Once, during the heady days of the Moscow summit, Nancy and I decided to break off from the entourage one afternoon to visit the shops on Arbat Street--that's a little street just off Moscow's main shopping area. Even though our visit was a surprise, every Russian there immediately recognized us and called out our names and reached for our hands. We were just about swept away by the warmth. You could almost feel the possibilities in all that joy. But within seconds, a KGB detail pushed their way toward us and began pushing and shoving the people in the crowd. It was an interesting moment. It reminded me that while the man on the street in the Soviet Union yearns for peace, the government is Communist. And those who run it are Communists, and that means we and they view such issues as freedom and human rights very differently.

We must keep up our guard, but we must also continue to work together to lessen and eliminate tension and mistrust. My view is that President Gorbachev is different from previous Soviet leaders. I think he knows some of the things wrong with his society and is trying to fix them. We wish him well. And we'll continue to work to make sure that the Soviet Union that eventually emerges from this process is a less threatening one. What it all boils down to is this: I want the new closeness to continue. And it will, as long as we make it clear that we will continue to act in a certain way as long as they continue to act in a helpful manner. If and when they don't, at first pull your punches. If they persist, pull the plug. It's still trust but verify. It's still play, but cut the cards. It's still watch closely. And don't be afraid to see what you see.

I've been asked if I have any regrets. Well, I do. The deficit is one. I've been talking a great deal about that lately, but tonight isn't for arguments, and I'm going to hold my tongue. But an observation: I've had my share of victories in the Congress, but what few people noticed is that I never won anything you didn't win for me. They never saw my troops, they never saw Reagan's regiments, the American people. You won every battle with every call you made and letter you wrote demanding action. Well, action is still needed. If we're to finish the job. Reagan's regiments will have to become the Bush brigades. Soon he'll be the chief, and he'll need you every bit as much as I did.

Finally, there is a great tradition of warnings in Presidential farewells, and I've got one that's been on my mind for some time. But oddly enough, it starts with one of the things I'm proudest of in the past 8 years: the resurgence of national pride that I called the new patriotism. This national feeling is good, but it won't count for much, and it won't last unless it's grounded in thoughtfulness and knowledge.

An informed patriotism is what we want. And are we doing a good enough job teaching our children what America is and what she represents in the long history of the world? Those of us who are over 35 or so years of age grew up in a different America. We were taught, very directly, what it means to be an American. And we absorbed, almost in the air, a love of country and an appreciation of its institutions. If you didn't get these things from your family, you got them from the neighborhood, from the father down the street who fought in Korea or the family who lost someone at Anzio. Or you could get a sense of patriotism from school. And if all else failed, you could get a sense of patriotism from the popular culture. The movies celebrated democratic values and implicitly reinforced the idea that America was special. TV was like that, too, through the mid-sixties.

But now, we're about to enter the nineties, and some things have changed. Younger parents aren't sure that an unambivalent appreciation of America is the right thing to teach modern children. And as for those who create the popular culture, well-grounded patriotism is no longer the style. Our spirit is back, but we haven't reinstitutionalized it. We've got to do a better job of getting across that America is freedom--freedom of speech, freedom of religion, freedom of enterprise. And freedom is special and rare. It's fragile; it needs [protection].

So, we've got to teach history based not on what's in fashion but what's important--why the Pilgrims came here, who Jimmy Doolittle was, and what those 30 seconds over Tokyo meant. You know, 4 years ago on the 40th anniversary of D-Day, I read a letter from a young woman writing to her late father, who'd fought on Omaha Beach. Her name was Lisa Zanatta Henn, and she said, "We will always remember, we will never forget what the boys of Normandy did." Well, let's help her keep her word. If we forget what we did, we won't know who we are. I'm warning of an eradication of the American memory that could result, ultimately, in an erosion of the American spirit. Let's start with some basics: more attention to American history and a greater emphasis on civic ritual.

And let me offer lesson number one about America: All great change in America begins at the dinner table. So, tomorrow night in the kitchen, I hope the talking begins. And children, if your parents haven't been teaching you what it means to be an American, let 'em know and nail 'em on it. That would be a very American thing to do.

And that's about all I have to say tonight, except for one thing. The past few days when I've been at that window upstairs, I've thought a bit of the "shining city upon a hill." The phrase comes from John Winthrop, who wrote it to describe the America he imagined. What he imagined was important because he was an early Pilgrim, an early freedom man. He journeyed here on what today we'd call a little wooden boat; and like the other Pilgrims, he was looking for a home that would be free. I've spoken of the shining city all my political life, but I don't know if I ever quite communicated what I saw when I said it. But in my mind it was a tall, proud city built on rocks stronger than oceans, windswept, God-blessed, and teeming with people of all kinds living in harmony and peace; a city with free ports that hummed with commerce and creativity. And if there had to be city walls, the walls had doors and the doors were open to anyone with the will and the heart to get here. That's how I saw it, and see it still.

And how stands the city on this winter night? More prosperous, more secure, and happier than it was 8 years ago. But more than that: After 200 years, two centuries, she still stands strong and true on the granite ridge, and her glow has held steady no matter what storm. And she's still a beacon, still a magnet for all who must have freedom, for all the pilgrims from all the lost places who are hurtling through the darkness, toward home.

We've done our part. And as I walk off into the city streets, a final word to the men and women of the Reagan revolution, the men and women across America who for 8 years did the work that brought America back. My friends: We did it. We weren't just marking time. We made a difference. We made the city stronger, we made the city freer, and we left her in good hands. All in all, not bad, not bad at all.

And so, goodbye, God bless you, and God bless the United States of America.

The Journey

Your America to be Free

June 7, 1957
Commencement Address at Eureka College

I'm sure you all must know the depth of my gratitude for this honor you have done me. What you can't know is how great is my feeling of unworthiness. For some 25 years I have nursed a feeling of guilt about the degree given me here upon the occasion of my own graduation. It was, I feel, more honorary than earned and for all these years I have carefully refrained from referring to myself as a "student" here. My very instinct is to mumble a modest "thanks" and sit down, but that retreat is denied me. Inherent in my invitation is the obligation to make some remarks appropriate to this occasion which shall climax your years of academic endeavor. I do not take this responsibility lightly. Realizing there are many present who are better qualified to perform this function, I have inquired right down to the start of the Processional as to an appropriate theme.

There was a temptation, of course, to beg your favor by citing the mistakes of my generation, dwelling on the awful state of the world and suggesting that you would bring order out of chaos and set things right. I'm not that pessimistic, however, and would be less than honest and sincere if I chose such a course. With your permission I would rather speak of something very close to my heart. You members of the graduating class of 1957 are today coming into your inheritance. You are taking your adult places in a society unique in the history of man's tribal relations. I would like to play the role of a "legal light" in the reading of the will, and to discuss with you the terms and conditions of your legacy.

Looming large in your inheritance is this country, this land America, placed as it is between two great oceans. Those who discovered and pioneered it had to have rare qualities of courage and imagination, nor did these qualities stop there. Even the modern-day immigrants have been possessed of courage beyond that of their neighbors. The courage to tear up centuries-old roots and leave their homelands, to come to this land where even the language was strange. Such courage is part of our inheritance, all of us spring from these special people and these qualities have contributed to the make-up of the American personality.

There are conditions to this "will" of which I speak. There are terms the heirs must meet in order to qualify for the legacy. But, I have never been able to believe that America is just a reward for those of extra courage and resourcefulness. This is a land of destiny and our forefathers found their way here by some Divine system of selective service gathered here to fulfill a mission to advance man a further step in his climb from the swamps.

Almost two centuries ago a group of disturbed men met in the small Pennsylvania State House [as] they gathered to decide on a course of action. Behind the locked and guarded doors they debated for hours whether or not to sign the Declaration which had been presented for their consideration. For hours the talk was treason and its price the headsman's axe, the gallows and noose. The talk went on and decision was not forthcoming. Then, Jefferson writes, a voice was heard coming from the balcony:

They may stretch our necks on all the gibbets in the land. They may turn every tree into a gallows, every home into a grave, and yet the words of that parchment can never die. They may pour our blood on a thousand scaffolds and yet from every drop that dyes the axe a new champion of freedom will spring into birth. The words of this declaration will live long after our bones are dust.

To the mechanic in his workshop they will speak hope; to the slave in the mines, freedom; but to the coward rulers, these words will speak in tones of warning they cannot help but hear. Sign that parchment. Sign if the next moment the noose is around your neck. Sign if the next minute this hall rings with the clash of falling axes! Sign by all your hopes in life or death, not only for yourselves but for all ages, for that parchment will be the textbook of freedom, the bible of the rights of man forever.

Were my soul trembling on the verge of eternity, my hand freezing in death, I would still implore you to remember this truth God has given America to be free.

As he finished, the speaker sank back in his seat exhausted. Inspired by his eloquence the delegates rushed forward to sign the Declaration of Independence. When they turned to thank the speaker for his timely words he couldn't be found and to this day no one knows who he was or how he entered or left the guarded room.

Here was the first challenge to the people of this new land, the charging of this nation with a responsibility to all mankind. And down through the years with but few lapses the people of America have fulfilled their destiny.

Almost a century and a half after that day in Philadelphia, this nation entered a great world conflict in Europe. Volumes of cynical words have been written about that war and our part in it. Our motives have been questioned and there has been talk of ulterior motives in high places, of world markets and balance of power. But all the words of all the cynics cannot erase the fact that millions of Americans sacrificed, fought and many died in the sincere and selfless belief that they were making the world safe for democracy and advancing the cause of freedom for all men.

A quarter of a century later America went into World War II, and never in the history of man had the issues of right and wrong been so clearly defined, so much so that it makes one question how anyone could have remained neutral. And again in the greatest mass undertaking the world has ever seen, America fulfilled her destiny.

A short time after that war was concluded a plane was winging its way across the Pacific Ocean. It contained dignitaries of the Philippines and of our own government. Landing at a naval installation a short distance from Manila, the plane was held there while those people listened by radio to the first detonation of an experimental atomic weapon at the Bikini Atoll. Then the plane took to the air again and soon landed in Manila. There these people, together with our vice president, senators, generals and admirals, met with 250,000 Philippines in the Grand Concourse, where they watched the American flag come down and the flag of the Philippine independence take its place.

I was privileged to sit in an auditorium one night and hear one of the passengers on that plane, a great man of the Philippines, describe this scene, General Carlos Romulo, whose father was killed by American soldiers in the Philippine insurrection. As a boy, the General was taught to be a guerrilla and to fight Americans and hate them. But I saw him, with tears in his eyes, tell us how he turned to his wife that day in Manila and said, "a hundred years from now will our children's children learn in their schoolrooms that on this day an atomic weapon was detonated for the first time on a Pacific Island, or will they learn that on another Pacific Island a great and powerful nation, which had bled the flower of its youth into the sands of the island's beaches reconquering them from a savage enemy, had on this day turned to the people of that island and for the first time in the history of man's relationship to man had said, 'Here, we've taken your country back for you. It's yours'." As we heard him, I think most of us realized once again the magnitude of the challenge of our destiny, that here indeed is "the last best hope of man on earth."

And now today we find ourselves involved in another struggle, this time called a cold war. This cold war between great sovereign nations isn't really a new struggle at all. It is the oldest struggle of human kind, as old as man himself. This is a simple struggle between those of us who believe that man has the dignity and sacred right and the ability to choose and shape his own destiny and those who do not so believe. This irreconcilable conflict is between those who believe in the sanctity of individual freedom and those who believe in the supremacy of the state.

In a phase of this struggle not widely known, some of us came toe to toe with this enemy this evil force in our own community in Hollywood, and make no mistake about it, this is an evil force. Don't be deceived because you are not hearing the sound of gunfire, because even so you are fighting for your lives. And you're fighting against the best organized and the most capable enemy of freedom and of right and decency that has ever been abroad in the world. Some years ago, back in the thirties, a man who was apparently just a technician came to Hollywood to take a job in our industry, an industry whose commerce is in tinsel and colored lights and make-believe. He went to work in the studios, and there were few to know he came to our town on direct orders from the Kremlin. When he quietly left our town a few years later the cells had been formed and planted in virtually all of our organizations, our guilds and unions. The framework for the Communist front organizations had been established.

It was some time later, under the guise of a jurisdictional strike involving a dispute between two unions, that we saw war come to Hollywood. Suddenly there were 5,000 tin-hatted, club-carrying pickets outside the studio gates. We saw some of our people caught by these hired henchmen; we saw them open car doors and put their arms across them and break them until they hung straight down the side of the car, and then these tin-hatted men would send our people on into the studio. We saw our so-called glamour girls, who certainly had to be conscious of what a scar on the face or a broken nose could mean careerwise going through those picket lines day after day without complaint. Nor did they falter when they found the bus which they used for transportation to and from work in flames from a bomb that had been thrown into it just before their arrival. Two blocks from the studio everyone would get down on hands and knees on the floor to avoid the bricks and stones coming through the windows. And the 5,000 pickets out there in their tin hats weren't even motion picture workers. They were maritime workers from the waterfront--members of Mr. Harry Bridges' union.

We won our fight in Hollywood, cleared them out after seven long months in which even homes were broken, months in which many of us carried arms that were granted us by the police, and in which policemen lived in our homes, guarding our children at night. And what of the quiet film technician who had left our town before the fighting started? Well, in 1951 he turned up on the Monterey Peninsula where he was involved in a union price-fixing conspiracy. Two years ago he appeared on the New York waterfront where he was Harry Bridges' right hand man in an attempt to establish a liaison between the New York and West Coast waterfront workers. And a few months ago he was mentioned in the speech of a U.S. Congresswoman who was thanking him for his help in framing labor legislation. He is a registered lobbyist in Washington for Harry Bridges.

Now that the first flush of victory is over we in Hollywood find ourselves blessed with a newly developed social awareness. We have allowed ourselves to become a sort of a village idiot on the fringe of the industrial scene, fair game for any demagogue or bigot who wants to stand up in the pulpit or platform and attack us. We are also fair game for those people, well-meaning though they may be, who believe that the answer to the world's ills is more government and more restraint and more regimentation. Suddenly we find that we are a group of second class citizens subject to discriminatory taxation, government interference and harassment.

This harassment reaches its peak, of course, in censorship. Here in this great land of the free, exchange of ideas in our section of the communications industry is subjected to political censorship in more than 200 cities and 11 states and it's spreading every day. But are we the only victims of these restraints and restrictions on our personal freedom? Is censorship really a restriction on us who already have a voluntary censorship code of good taste, or is this an invasion of your freedom? Isn't this the case of a few of your neighbors taking it upon themselves the right to tell you what you are capable of seeing and hearing on a motion picture screen?

So we worry a little about the class of '57, we who are older and have known another day. We worry that perhaps someday you might not resist as strongly as we would if someone decides to tell you what you can read in a newspaper, or hear on the radio, or hear from a speaker's platform, or what you can say or what you can think. So there are terms and conditions to the will, and one of the terms is your own eternal vigilance guarding against restrictions on our American freedom.

You today are smarter than we were. You are better educated and better informed than we were twenty-five years ago. And that is part of your heritage. You enjoy these added benefits because, more than 100 years ago near this very spot, a man plunged an ax into a tree and said, "here we will build a school for our children." And for over 100 years people have contributed to the endowment and support of this college. Their contributions were of the utmost in generosity because they could never know the handclasp of gratitude in return for their contributions. Their gifts were to generations yet unborn.

Many of us here share this heritage with you, and some of us shared it under different circumstances. I recall my own days on this campus in the depths of the depression. Even with study and reading I don't think you can quite understand what it was like to live in an America where the Illinois National Guard, with fixed bayonets, paraded down Michigan Avenue in Chicago as a warning to the more than half million unemployed men who slept every night in alleys and doorways under newspapers. On this campus many of us came who brought not one cent to help this school and pay for our education. The college, of course, had suffered and lost much of its endowment in the stock crash, had seen its revenue not only from endowment but from gifts curtailed because of the great financial chaos. But we heard none of that. We attended a college that made it possible for us to attend regardless of our lack of means, that created jobs for us, so that we could eat and sleep, and that allowed us to defer our tuition and trusted that they could get paid some day long after we had gone. And the professors, God bless them, on this campus, the most dedicated group of men and women whom I have ever known, went long months without drawing any pay. Sometimes the college, with a donation of a little money or produce from a farm, would buy groceries and dole them out to the teachers to at least try and provide them with food. We know something of your heritage, but even if we had been able to pay as many of you have paid for your education we, and you, must realize that the total price paid by any student of this college is far less than it costs this college to educate you. This is true not only of Eureka, but of the hundreds of schools and universities across the land.

Now today as you prepare to leave your Alma Mater, you go into a world in which, due to our carelessness and apathy, a great many of our freedoms have been lost. It isn't that an outside enemy has taken them. It's just that there is something inherent in government which makes it, when it isn't controlled, continue to grow. So today for every seven of us sitting here in this lovely outdoor theater, there is one public servant, and 31 cents of every dollar earned in America goes in taxes. To support the multitudinous and gigantic functions of government, taxation is levied which tends to dry up the very sources of contributions and donations to colleges like Eureka. So in this time of prosperity we find these church schools, these small independent colleges and even the larger universities, hard put to maintain themselves and to continue doing the job they have done so unselfishly and well for all these years. Observe the contrast between these small church colleges and our government, because, as I have said before, these have always given far more than was ever given to them in return.

Class of 1957, it will be part of the terms of the will for you to take stock in the days to come, because we enjoy a form of government in which mistakes can be rectified. The dictator can never admit he was wrong, but we are blessed with a form of government where we can call a halt, and say, "Back up. Let's take another look." Remember that every government service, every offer of government financed security, is paid for in the loss of personal freedom. I am not castigating government and business for those many areas of normal cooperation, for those services that we know we must have and that we do willingly support. It is very easy to give up our personal freedom to drive 90 miles an hour down a city street in return for the safety that we will get for ourselves and our loved ones. Of course, that might not be a good example, it seems sometimes that this is a thing we have paid for in advance and the merchandise hasn't yet been delivered. But in the days to come whenever a voice is raised telling you to let the government do it, analyze very carefully to see whether the suggested service is worth the personal freedom which you must forego in return for such service.

There are many well-meaning people today who work at placing an economic floor beneath all of us so that no one shall exist below a certain level or standard of living, and certainly we don't quarrel with this. But look more closely and you may find that all too often these well-meaning people are building a ceiling above which no one shall be permitted to climb and between the two are pressing us all into conformity, into a mold of standardized mediocrity. The tendency toward assembly-line education in some of our larger institutions, where we are not teaching but training to fulfill certain specific jobs in the economic life of our nation, is a part of this same pattern.

We have a vast system of public education in this country, a network of great state universities and colleges and none of us would have it otherwise. But there are those among us who urge expansion of this system until all education is by way of tax-supported institutions. Today we enjoy academic freedom in America as it is enjoyed nowhere else in the world. But this pattern was established by the independent secular and church colleges of our land, schools like Eureka. Down through the years these colleges and universities have maintained intellectual freedom because they were beholden to no political group, for when politics control the purse strings, they also control the policy. No one advocates the elimination of our tax-supported universities, but we should never forget that their academic freedom is assured only so long as we have the leavening influence of hundreds of privately endowed colleges and universities throughout the land.

So you should resolve, here and now, that you will not only accept your heritage but abide by the terms and conditions of the will. You should firmly resolve that these schools will not just be a part of America's past, but that they will continue to be a part of America's great future. Democracy with the personal freedoms that are ours we hold literally in trust for that day when we shall have fulfilled our destiny and brought mankind a great and long step from the swamps. Can we deliver it to our children? Democracy depends upon service voluntarily rendered, money voluntarily contributed.

These institutions which have contributed so much to us, from which we have received so much of our heritage, were here for our benefit only because our forefathers preferred voluntarily to support institutions of their choice in addition to sharing taxation for the support of governmental institutions. The will provides, class of 1957, not only that you receive this heritage and cherish it, but that you voluntarily tax your own time and your own money and contribute to these free institutions so that generations not yet born in this country and in the rest of the world, may benefit from this same heritage of freedom.

It will be very easy for you to say, "Well, I will do something, some day. When I can afford it, I am going to." But would you let an old "grad" tell you one thing now? Giving is a habit. Get into the habit now, because you will never be able to afford to give and contribute, thus to repay the obligation you owe to those people who made this college possible, if you wait until you think you can afford it. Start now regardless of how small, and in the days to come when you are confronted with demands for many worthwhile causes and charities I think you will find that you will give dutifully to all the worthy ones. But here and there you will pick one or two that will be favorites, and you can do no better than to pick this, your Alma Mater, because you will not only be repaying your own personal obligations, you will be making your contribution to the very process which has made and continues to keep America great.

This democracy of ours which sometimes we've treated so lightly, is more than ever a comfortable cloak, so let us not tear it asunder, for no man knows once it is destroyed where or when he will find its protective warmth again.

A Time for Choosing

October 27, 1964

I am going to talk of controversial things. I make no apology for this.

It's time we asked ourselves if we still know the freedoms intended for us by the Founding Fathers. James Madison said, "We base all our experiments on the capacity of mankind for self government."

This idea -- that government was beholden to the people, that it had no other source of power -- is still the newest, most unique idea in all the long history of man's relation to man. This is the issue of this election: Whether we believe in our capacity for self-government or whether we abandon the American Revolution and confess that a little intellectual elite in a far-distant capital can plan our lives for us better than we can plan them ourselves.

You and I are told we must choose between a left or right, but I suggest there is no such thing as a left or right. There is only an up or down. Up to man's age-old dream--the maximum of individual freedom consistent with order -- or down to the ant heap of totalitarianism. Regardless of their sincerity, their humanitarian motives, those who would sacrifice freedom for security have embarked on this downward path. Plutarch warned, "The real destroyer of the liberties of the people is he who spreads among them bounties, donations and benefits."

The Founding Fathers knew a government can't control the economy without controlling people. And they knew when a government sets out to do that, it must use force and coercion to achieve its purpose. So we have come to a time for choosing.

Public servants say, always with the best of intentions, "What greater service we could render if only we had a little more money and a little more power." But the truth is that outside of its legitimate function, government does nothing as well or as economically as the private sector.

Yet any time you and I question the schemes of the do-gooders, we're denounced as being opposed to their humanitarian goals. It seems impossible to legitimately debate their solutions with the assumption that all of us share the desire to help the less fortunate. They tell us we're always "against," never "for" anything.

We are for a provision that destitution should not follow unemployment by reason of old age, and to that end we have accepted Social Security as a step toward meeting the problem. However, we are against those entrusted with this program when they practice deception regarding its fiscal shortcomings, when they charge that any criticism of the program means that we want to end payments....

We are for aiding our allies by sharing our material blessings with nations which share our fundamental beliefs, but we are against doling out money government to government, creating bureaucracy, if not socialism, all over the world.

We need true tax reform that will at least make a start toward restoring for our children the American Dream that wealth is denied to no one, that each individual has the right to fly as high as his strength and ability will take him.... But we cannot have such reform while our tax policy is engineered by people who view the tax as a means of achieving changes in our social structure....

Have we the courage and the will to face up to the immorality and discrimination of the progressive tax, and demand a return to traditional proportionate taxation? . . . Today in our country the tax collector's share is 37 cents of every dollar earned. Freedom has never been so fragile, so close to slipping from our grasp.

Are you willing to spend time studying the issues, making yourself aware, and then conveying that information to family and friends? Will you resist the temptation to get a government handout for your community? Realize that the doctor's fight against socialized medicine is your fight. We can't socialize the doctors without socializing the patients. Recognize that government invasion of public power is eventually an assault upon your own business. If some among you fear taking a stand because you are afraid of reprisals from customers, clients, or even government, recognize that you are just feeding the crocodile hoping he'll eat you last.

If all of this seems like a great deal of trouble, think what's at stake. We are faced with the most evil enemy mankind has known in his long climb from the swamp to the stars. There can be no security anywhere in the free world if there is no fiscal and economic stability within the United States. Those who ask us to trade our freedom for the soup kitchen of the welfare state are architects of a policy of accommodation.

They say the world has become too complex for simple answers. They are wrong. There are no easy answers, but there are simple answers. We must have the courage to do what we know is morally right. Winston Churchill said that "the destiny of man is not measured by material computation. When great forces are on the move in the world, we learn we are spirits--not animals." And he said, "There is something going on in time and space, and beyond time and space, which, whether we like it or not, spells duty."

You and I have a rendezvous with destiny. We will preserve for our children this, the last best hope of man on earth, or we will sentence them to take the first step into a thousand years of darkness. If we fail, at least let our children and our children's children say of us we justified our brief moment here. We did all that could be done.

We Will Be a City Upon a Hill

January 25, 1974
First Conservative Political Action Conference

There are three men here tonight I am very proud to introduce. It was a year ago this coming February when this country had its spirits lifted as they have never been lifted in many years. This happened when planes began landing on American soil and in the Philippines, bringing back men who had lived with honor for many miserable years in North Vietnam prisons. Three of those men are here tonight, John McCain, Bill Lawrence and Ed Martin. It is an honor to be here tonight. I am proud that you asked me and I feel more than a little humble in the presence of this distinguished company.

There are men here tonight who, through their wisdom, their foresight and their courage, have earned the right to be regarded as prophets of our philosophy. Indeed they are prophets of our times. In years past when others were silent or too blind to the facts, they spoke up forcefully and fearlessly for what they believed to be right. A decade has passed since Barry Goldwater walked a lonely path across this land reminding us that even a land as rich as ours can't go on forever borrowing against the future, leaving a legacy of debt for another generation and causing a runaway inflation to erode the savings and reduce the standard of living. Voices have been raised trying to rekindle in our country all of the great ideas and principles which set this nation apart from all the others that preceded it, but louder and more strident voices utter easily sold cliches.

Cartoonists with acid-tipped pens portray some of the reminders of our heritage and our destiny as old-fashioned. They say that we are trying to retreat into a past that actually never existed. Looking to the past in an effort to keep our country from repeating the errors of history is termed by them as "taking the country back to McKinley." Of course, I never found that was so bad -- under McKinley we freed Cuba. On the span of history, we are still thought of as a young upstart country celebrating soon only our second century as a nation, and yet we are the oldest continuing republic in the world.

I thought that tonight, rather than talking on the subjects you are discussing, or trying to find something new to say, it might be appropriate to reflect a bit on our heritage.

You can call it mysticism if you want to, but I have always believed that there was some divine plan that placed this great continent between two oceans to be sought out by those who were possessed of an abiding love of freedom and a special kind of courage.

This was true of those who pioneered the great wilderness in the beginning of this country, as it is also true of those later immigrants who were willing to leave the land of their birth and come to a land where even the language was unknown to them. Call it chauvinistic, but our heritage does set us apart. Some years ago a writer, who happened to be an avid student of history, told me a story about that day in the little hall in Philadelphia where honorable men, hard-pressed by a King who was flouting the very law they were willing to obey, debated whether they should take the fateful step of declaring their independence from that king. I was told by this man that the story could be found in the writings of Jefferson. I confess, I never researched or made an effort to verify it. Perhaps it is only legend. But story, or legend, he described the atmosphere, the strain, the debate, and that as men for the first time faced the consequences of such an irretrievable act, the walls resounded with the dread word of treason and its price -- the gallows and the headman's axe. As the day wore on the issue hung in the balance, and then, according to the story, a man rose in the small gallery. He was not a young man and was obviously calling on all the energy he could muster. Citing the grievances that had brought them to this moment, he said, "Sign that parchment. They may turn every tree into a gallows, every home into a grave and yet the words of that parchment can never die. For the mechanic in his workshop, they will be words of hope, to the slave in the mines -- freedom." And he added, "If my hands were freezing in death, I would sign that parchment with my last ounce of strength. Sign, sign if the next moment the noose is around your neck, sign even if the hall is ringing with the sound of headman's axe, for that parchment will be the textbook of freedom, the bible of the rights of man forever." And then it is said he fell back exhausted. But 56 delegates, swept by his eloquence, signed the Declaration of Independence, a document destined to be as immortal as any work of man can be. And according to the story, when they turned to thank him for his timely oratory, he could not be found nor were there any who knew who he was or how he had come in or gone out through the locked and guarded doors.

Well, as I say, whether story or legend, the signing of the document that day in Independence Hall was miracle enough. Fifty-six men, a little band so unique -- we have never seen their like since -- pledged their lives, their fortunes and their sacred honor. Sixteen gave their lives, most gave their fortunes and all of them preserved their sacred honor. What manner of men were they? Certainly they were not an unwashed, revolutionary rabble, nor were they adventurers in a heroic mood. Twenty-four were lawyers and jurists, 11 were merchants and tradesmen, nine were farmers. They were men who would achieve security but valued freedom more.

And what price did they pay? John Hart was driven from the side of his desperately ill wife. After more than a year of living almost as an animal in the forest and in caves, he returned to find his wife had died and his children had vanished. He never saw them again, his property was destroyed and he died of a broken heart -- but with no regret, only pride in the part he had played that day in Independence Hall. Carter Braxton of Virginia lost all his ships -- they were sold to pay his debts. He died in rags. So it was with Ellery, Clymer, Hall, Walton, Gwinnett, Rutledge, Morris, Livingston, and Middleton. Nelson, learning that Cornwallis was using his home for a headquarters, personally begged Washington to fire on him and destroy his home--he died bankrupt. It has never been reported that any of these men ever expressed bitterness or renounced their action as not worth the price. Fifty-six rank-and-file, ordinary citizens had founded a nation that grew from sea to shining sea, five million farms, quiet villages, cities that never sleep -- all done without an area re-development plan, urban renewal or a rural legal assistance program.

Now we are a nation of 211 million people with a pedigree that includes blood lines from every corner of the world. We have shed that American-melting-pot blood in every corner of the world, usually in defense of someone's freedom. Those who remained of that remarkable band we call our Founding Fathers tied up some of the loose ends about a dozen years after the Revolution. It had been the first revolution in all man's history that did not just exchange one set of rulers for another. This had been a philosophical revolution. The culmination of men's dreams for 6,000 years were formalized with the Constitution, probably the most unique document ever drawn in the long history of man's relation to man. I know there have been other constitutions, new ones are being drawn today by newly emerging nations. Most of them, even the one of the Soviet Union, contain many of the same guarantees as our own Constitution, and still there is a difference. The difference is so subtle that we often overlook it, but it is so great that it tells the whole story. Those other constitutions say, "Government grants you these rights," and ours says, "You are born with these rights, they are yours by the grace of God, and no government on earth can take them from you."

Lord Acton of England, who once said, "Power corrupts, and absolute power corrupts absolutely," would say of that document, "They had solved with astonishing ease and unduplicated success two problems which had heretofore baffled the capacity of the most enlightened nations. They had contrived a system of federal government which prodigiously increased national power and yet respected local liberties and authorities, and they had founded it on a principle of equality without surrendering the securities of property or freedom." Never in any society has the preeminence of the individual been so firmly established and given such a priority.

In less than twenty years we would go to war because the God-given rights of the American sailors, as defined in the Constitution, were being violated by a foreign power. We served notice then on the world that all of us together would act collectively to safeguard the rights of even the least among us. But still, in an older, cynical world, they were not convinced. The great powers of Europe still had the idea that one day this great continent would be open again to colonizing and they would come over and divide us up.

In the meantime, men who yearned to breathe free were making their way to our shores. Among them was a young refugee from the Austro-Hungarian Empire. He had been a leader in an attempt to free Hungary from Austrian rule. The attempt had failed and he fled to escape execution. In America, this young Hungarian, Koscha by name, became an importer by trade and took out his first citizenship papers. One day, business took him to a Mediterranean port. There was a large Austrian warship under the command of an admiral in the harbor. He had a manservant with him. He had described to this manservant what the flag of his new country looked like. Word was passed to the Austrian warship that this revolutionary was there and in the night he was kidnapped and taken aboard that large ship. This man's servant, desperate, walking up and down the harbor, suddenly spied a flag that resembled the description he had heard. It was a small American war sloop. He went aboard and told Captain Ingraham, of that war sloop, his story. Captain Ingraham went to the American Consul. When the American Consul learned that Koscha had only taken out his first citizenship papers, the consul washed his hands of the incident. Captain Ingraham said, "I am the senior officer in this port and I believe, under my oath of my office, that I owe this man the protection of our flag."

He went aboard the Austrian warship and demanded to see their prisoner, our citizen. The Admiral was amused, but they brought the man on deck. He was in chains and had been badly beaten.

Captain Ingraham said, "I can hear him better without those chains," and the chains were removed. He walked over and said to Koscha, "I will ask you one question; consider your answer carefully. Do you ask the protection of the American flag?" Koscha nodded dumbly, "Yes," and the Captain said, "You shall have it." He went back and told the frightened consul what he had done. Later in the day three more Austrian ships sailed into harbor. It looked as though the four were getting ready to leave. Captain Ingraham sent a junior officer over to the Austrian flag ship to tell the Admiral that any attempt to leave that harbor with our citizen aboard would be resisted with appropriate force. He said that he would expect a satisfactory answer by four o'clock that afternoon. As the hour neared they looked at each other through the glasses. As it struck four he had them roll the cannons into the ports and had them light the tapers with which they would set off the cannons -- one little sloop. Suddenly the lookout tower called out and said, "They are lowering a boat," and they rowed Koscha over to the little American ship.

Captain Ingraham then went below and wrote his letter of resignation to the United States Navy. In it he said, "I did what I thought my oath of office required, but if I have embarrassed my country in any way, I resign." His resignation was refused in the United States Senate with these words: "This battle that was never fought may turn out to be the most important battle in our Nation's history." Incidentally, there is to this day, and I hope there always will be, a USS Ingraham in the United States Navy.

I did not tell that story out of any desire to be narrowly chauvinistic or to glorify aggressive militarism, but it is an example of government meeting its highest responsibility.

In recent years we have been treated to a rash of noble-sounding phrases. Some of them sound good, but they don't hold up under close analysis. Take for instance the slogan so frequently uttered by the young senator from Massachusetts, "The greatest good for the greatest number." Certainly under that slogan, no modern day Captain Ingraham would risk even the smallest craft and crew for a single citizen. Every dictator who ever lived has justified the enslavement of his people on the theory of what was good for the majority.

We are not a warlike people. Nor is our history filled with tales of aggressive adventures and imperialism, which might come as a shock to some of the placard painters in our modern demonstrations. The lesson of Vietnam, I think, should be that never again will young Americans be asked to fight and possibly die for a cause unless that cause is so meaningful that we, as a nation, pledge our full resources to achieve victory as quickly as possible.

I realize that such a pronouncement, of course, would possibly be laying one open to the charge of warmongering -- but that would also be ridiculous. My generation has paid a higher price and has fought harder for freedom than any generation that had ever lived. We have known four wars in a single lifetime. All were horrible, all could have been avoided if at a particular moment in time we had made it plain that we subscribed to the words of John Stuart Mill when he said that "war is an ugly thing, but not the ugliest of things."

The decayed and degraded state of moral and patriotic feeling which thinks nothing is worth a war is worse. The man who has nothing which he cares about more than his personal safety is a miserable creature and has no chance of being free unless made and kept so by the exertions of better men than himself.

The widespread disaffection with things military is only a part of the philosophical division in our land today. I must say to you who have recently, or presently are still receiving an education, I am awed by your powers of resistance. I have some knowledge of the attempts that have been made in many classrooms and lecture halls to persuade you that there is little to admire in America. For the second time in this century, capitalism and the free enterprise are under assault. Privately owned business is blamed for spoiling the environment, exploiting the worker and seducing, if not outright raping, the customer. Those who make the charge have the solution, of course -- government regulation and control. We may never get around to explaining how citizens who are so gullible that they can be suckered into buying cereal or soap that they don't need and would not be good for them, can at the same time be astute enough to choose representatives in government to which they would entrust the running of their lives.

Not too long ago, a poll was taken on 2,500 college campuses in this country. Thousands and thousands of responses were obtained. Overwhelmingly, 65, 70, and 75 percent of the students found business responsible, as I have said before, for the things that were wrong in this country. That same number said that government was the solution and should take over the management and the control of private business. Eighty percent of the respondents said they wanted government to keep its paws out of their private lives.

We are told every day that the assembly-line worker is becoming a dull-witted robot and that mass production results in standardization. Well, there isn't a socialist country in the world that would not give its copy of Karl Marx for our standardization.

Standardization means production for the masses and the assembly line means more leisure for the worker -- freedom from backbreaking and mind-dulling drudgery that man had known for centuries past. Karl Marx did not abolish child labor or free the women from working in the coal mines in England – the steam engine and modern machinery did that.

Unfortunately, the disciples of the new order have had a hand in determining too much policy in recent decades. Government has grown in size and power and cost through the New Deal, the Fair Deal, the New Frontier and the Great Society. It costs more for government today than a family pays for food, shelter and clothing combined. Not even the Office of Management and Budget knows how many boards, commissions, bureaus and agencies there are in the federal government, but the federal registry, listing their regulations, is just a few pages short of being as big as the Encyclopedia Britannica.

During the Great Society we saw the greatest growth of this government. There were eight cabinet departments and 12 independent agencies to administer the federal health program. There were 35 housing programs and 20 transportation projects. Public utilities had to cope with 27 different agencies on just routine business. There were 192 installations and nine departments with 1,000 projects having to do with the field of pollution.

One Congressman found the federal government was spending 4 billion dollars on research in its own laboratories but did not know where they were, how many people were working in them, or what they were doing. One of the research projects was "The Demography of Happiness," and for 249,000 dollars we found that "people who make more money are happier than people who make less, young people are happier than old people, and people who are healthier are happier than people who are sick." For 15 cents they could have bought an Almanac and read the old bromide, "It's better to be rich, young and healthy, than poor, old and sick."

The course that you have chosen is far more in tune with the hopes and aspirations of our people than are those who would sacrifice freedom for some fancied security.

Standing on the tiny deck of the Arabella in 1630 off the Massachusetts coast, John Winthrop said, "We will be as a city upon a hill. The eyes of all people are upon us, so that if we deal falsely with our God in this work we have undertaken and so cause Him to withdraw His present help from us, we shall be made a story and a byword throughout the world." Well, we have not dealt falsely with our God, even if He is temporarily suspended from the classroom.

When I was born my life expectancy was 10 years less than I have already lived – that's a cause of regret for some people in California, I know. Ninety percent of Americans at that time lived beneath what is considered the poverty line today, three-quarters lived in what is considered substandard housing. Today each of those figures is less than 10 percent. We have increased our life expectancy by wiping out, almost totally, diseases that still ravage mankind in other parts of the world. I doubt if the young people here tonight know the names of some of the diseases that were commonplace when we were growing up. We have more doctors per thousand people than any nation in the world. We have more hospitals than any nation in the world.

When I was your age, believe it or not, none of us knew that we even had a racial problem. When I graduated from college and became a radio sport announcer, broadcasting major league baseball, I didn't have a Hank Aaron or a Willie Mays to talk about. The Spaulding Guide said baseball was a game for Caucasian gentlemen. Some of us then began editorializing and campaigning against this. Gradually we campaigned against all those other areas where the constitutional rights of a large segment of our citizenry were being denied. We have not finished the job. We still have a long way to go, but we have made more progress in a few years than we have made in more than a century.

One-third of all the students in the world who are pursuing higher education are doing so in the United States. The percentage of our young Negro community that is going to college is greater than the percentage of whites in any other country in the world.

One-half of all the economic activity in the entire history of man has taken place in this republic. We have distributed our wealth more widely among our people than any society known to man. Americans work less hours for a higher standard of living than any other people. Ninety-five percent of all our families have an adequate daily intake of nutrients -- and a part of the five percent that don't are trying to lose weight! Ninety-nine percent have gas or electric refrigeration, 92 percent have televisions, and an equal number have telephones. There are 120 million cars on our streets and highways -- and all of them are on the street at once when you are trying to get home at night. But isn't this just proof of our materialism -- the very thing that we are charged with? Well, we also have more churches, more libraries, we support voluntarily more symphony orchestras, and opera companies, non-profit theaters, and publish more books than all the other nations of the world put together.

Somehow America has bred a kindliness into our people unmatched anywhere, as has been pointed out in that best-selling record by a Canadian journalist. We are not a sick society. A sick society could not produce the men that set foot on the moon, or who are now circling the earth above us in the Skylab. A sick society bereft of morality and courage did not produce the men who went through those years of torture and captivity in Vietnam. Where did we find such men? They are typical of this land as the Founding Fathers were typical. We found them in our streets, in the offices, the shops and the working places of our country and on the farms.

We cannot escape our destiny, nor should we try to do so. The leadership of the free world was thrust upon us two centuries ago in that little hall of Philadelphia. In the days following World War II, when the economic strength and power of America was all that stood between the world and the return to the dark ages, Pope Pius XII said, "The American people have a great genius for splendid and unselfish actions. Into the hands of America God has placed the destinies of an afflicted mankind."

We are indeed, and we are today, the last best hope of man on earth.

Let Them Go Their Way

March 1, 1975
2nd Annual CPAC Convention

Since our last meeting we have been through a disastrous election. It is easy for us to be discouraged, as pundits hail that election as a repudiation of our philosophy and even as a mandate of some kind or other. But the significance of the election was not registered by those who voted, but by those who stayed home. If there was anything like a mandate it will be found among almost two-thirds of the citizens who refused to participate.

Bitter as it is to accept the results of the November election, we should have reason for some optimism. For many years now we have preached "the gospel," in opposition to the philosophy of so-called liberalism which was, in truth, a call to collectivism.

Now, it is possible we have been persuasive to a greater degree than we had ever realized. Few, if any, Democratic party candidates in the last election ran as liberals. Listening to them I had the eerie feeling we were hearing reruns of Goldwater speeches. I even thought I heard a few of my own.

Bureaucracy was assailed and fiscal responsibility hailed. Even George McGovern donned sackcloth and ashes and did penance for the good people of South Dakota.

But let's not be so naive as to think we are witnessing a mass conversion to the principles of conservatism. Once sworn into office, the victors reverted to type. In their view, apparently, the ends justified the means.

The "Young Turks" had campaigned against "evil politicians." They turned against committee chairmen of their own party, displaying a taste and talent as cutthroat power politicians quite in contrast to their campaign rhetoric and idealism. Still, we must not forget that they molded their campaigning to fit what even they recognized was the mood of the majority. And we must see to it that the people are reminded of this as they now pursue their ideological goals -- and pursue them they will.

I know you are aware of the national polls which show that a greater (and increasing) number of Americans -- Republicans, Democrats and independents -- classify themselves as "conservatives" than ever before. And a poll of rank-and-file union members reveals dissatisfaction with the amount of power their own leaders have assumed, and a resentment of their use of that power for partisan politics. Would it shock you to know that in that poll 68 percent of rank-and-file union members of this country came out endorsing right-to-work legislation?

These polls give cause for some optimism, but at the same time reveal a confusion that exists and the need for a continued effort to "spread the word."

In another recent survey, of 35,000 college and university students polled, three-fourths blame American business and industry for all of our economic and social ills. The same three-fourths think the answer is more (and virtually complete) regimentation and government control of all phases of business -- including the imposition of wage and price controls. Yet, 80 percent in the same poll want less government interference in their own lives!

In 1972 the people of this country had a clear-cut choice, based on the issues -- to a greater extent than any election in half a century. In overwhelming numbers they ignored party labels, not so much to vote for a man or even a policy as to repudiate a philosophy. In doing so they repudiated that final step into the welfare state -- that call for the confiscation and redistribution of their earnings on a scale far greater than what we now have. They repudiated the abandonment of national honor and a weakening of this nation's ability to protect itself.

A study has been made that is so revealing that I'm not surprised it has been ignored by a certain number of political commentators and columnists. The political science department of Georgetown University researched the mandate of the 1972 election and recently presented its findings at a seminar.

Taking several major issues which, incidentally, are still the issues of the day, they polled rank-and-file members of the Democratic party on their approach to these problems. Then they polled the delegates to the two major national conventions -- the leaders of the parties.

They found the delegates to the Republican convention almost identical in their responses to those of the rank-and-file Republicans. Yet, the delegates to the Democratic convention were miles apart from the thinking of their own party members.

The mandate of 1972 still exists. The people of America have been confused and disturbed by events since that election, but they hold an unchanged philosophy.

Our task is to make them see that what we represent is identical to their own hopes and dreams of what America can and should be. If there are questions as to whether the principles of conservatism hold up in practice, we have the answers to them. Where conservative principles have been tried, they have worked. Gov. Meldrim Thomson is making them work in New Hampshire; so is Arch Moore in West Virginia and Mills Godwin in Virginia. Jack Williams made them work in Arizona and I'm sure Jim Edwards will in South Carolina.

If you will permit me, I can recount my own experience in California.

When I went to Sacramento eight years ago, I had the belief that government was no deep, dark mystery, that it could be operated efficiently by using the same common sense practiced in our everyday life, in our homes, in business and private affairs.

The "lab test" of my theory – California -- was pretty messed up after eight years of a road show version of the Great Society. Our first and only briefing came from the outgoing director of finance, who said: "We're spending $1 million more a day than we're taking in. I have a golf date. Good luck!" That was the most cheerful news we were to hear for quite some time.

California state government was increasing by about 5,000 new employees a year. We were the welfare capital of the world with 16 percent of the nation's caseload. Soon, California's caseload was increasing by 40,000 a month.

We turned to the people themselves for help. Two hundred and fifty experts in the various fields volunteered to serve on task forces at no cost to the taxpayers. They went into every department of state government and came back with 1,800 recommendations on how modern business practices could be used to make government more efficient. We adopted 1,600 of them.

We instituted a policy of "cut, squeeze and trim" and froze the hiring of employees as replacements for retiring employees or others leaving state service.

After a few years of struggling with the professional welfarists, we again turned to the people. First, we obtained another task force and, when the legislature refused to help implement its recommendations, we presented the recommendations to the electorate.

It still took some doing. The legislature insisted our reforms would not work; that the needy would starve in the streets; that the workload would be dumped on the counties; that property taxes would go up and that we'd run up a deficit the first year of $750 million.

That was four years ago. Today, the needy have had an average increase of 43 percent in welfare grants in California, but the taxpayers have saved $2 billion by the caseload not increasing that 40,000 a month. Instead, there are some 400,000 fewer on welfare today than then.

Forty of the state's 58 counties have reduced property taxes for two years in a row (some for three). That $750-million deficit turned into an $850-million surplus which we returned to the people in a one-time tax rebate. That wasn't easy. One state senator described that rebate as "an unnecessary expenditure of public funds."

For more than two decades governments -- federal, state, local -- have been increasing in size two-and-a-half times faster than the population increase. In the last 10 years they have increased the cost in payroll seven times as fast as the increase in numbers.

We have just turned over to a new administration in Sacramento a government virtually the same size it was eight years ago. With the state's growth rate, this means that government absorbed a workload increase, in some departments as much as 66 percent.

We also turned over -- for the first time in almost a quarter of a century -- a balanced budget and a surplus of $500 million. In these eight years just passed, we returned to the people in rebates, tax reductions and bridge toll reductions $5.7 billion. All of this is contrary to the will of those who deplore conservatism and profess to be liberals, yet all of it is pleasing to its citizenry.

Make no mistake, the leadership of the Democratic party is still out of step with the majority of Americans.

Speaker Carl Albert recently was quoted as saying that our problem is "60 percent recession, 30 percent inflation and 10 percent energy." That makes as much sense as saying two and two make 22.

Without inflation there would be no recession. And unless we curb inflation we can see the end of our society and economic system. The painful fact is we can only halt inflation by undergoing a period of economic dislocation -- a recession, if you will.

We can take steps to ease the suffering of some who will be hurt more than others, but if we turn from fighting inflation and adopt a program only to fight recession we are on the road to disaster.

In his first address to Congress, the president asked Congress to join him in an all-out effort to balance the budget. I think all of us wish that he had re-issued that speech instead of this year's budget message.

What side can be taken in a debate over whether the deficit should be $52 billion or $70 billion or $80 billion preferred by the profligate Congress?

Inflation has one cause and one cause only: government spending more than government takes in. And the cure to inflation is a balanced budget. We know, of course, that after 40 years of social tinkering and Keynesian experimentation that we can't do this all at once, but it can be achieved. Balancing the budget is like protecting your virtue: you have to learn to say "no."

This is no time to repeat the shopworn panaceas of the New Deal, the Fair Deal and the Great Society. John Kenneth Galbraith, who, in my opinion, is living proof that economics is an inexact science, has written a new book. It is called "Economics and the Public Purpose." In it, he asserts that market arrangements in our economy have given us inadequate housing, terrible mass transit, poor health care and a host of other miseries. And then, for the first time to my knowledge, he advances socialism as the answer to our problems.

Shorn of all side issues and extraneous matter, the problem underlying all others is the worldwide contest for the hearts and minds of mankind. Do we find the answers to human misery in freedom as it is known, or do we sink into the deadly dullness of the Socialist ant heap?

Those who suggest that the latter is some kind of solution are, I think, open to challenge. Let's have no more theorizing when actual comparison is possible. There is in the world a great nation, larger than ours in territory and populated with 250 million capable people. It is rich in resources and has had more than 50 uninterrupted years to practice socialism without opposition.

We could match them, but it would take a little doing on our part. We'd have to cut our paychecks back by 75 percent; move 60 million workers back to the farm; abandon two-thirds of our steel-making capacity; destroy 40 million television sets; tear up 14 of every 15 miles of highway; junk 19 of every 20 automobiles; tear up two-thirds of our railroad track; knock down 70 percent of our houses; and rip out nine out of every 10 telephones. Then, all we have to do is find a capitalist country to sell us wheat on credit to keep us from starving!

Our people are in a time of discontent. Our vital energy supplies are threatened by possibly the most powerful cartel in human history. Our traditional allies in Western Europe are experiencing political and economic instability bordering on chaos.

We seem to be increasingly alone in a world grown more hostile, but we let our defenses shrink to pre-Pearl Harbor levels. And we are conscious that in Moscow the crash build-up of arms continues. The SALT II agreement in Vladivostok, if not re-negotiated, guarantees the Soviets a clear missile superiority sufficient to make a "first strike" possible, with little fear of reprisal. Yet, too many congressmen demand further cuts in our own defenses, including delay if not cancellation of the B-1 bomber.

I realize that millions of Americans are sick of hearing about Indochina, and perhaps it is politically unwise to talk of our obligation to Cambodia and South Vietnam. But we pledged -- in an agreement that brought our men home and freed our prisoners -- to give our allies arms and ammunition to replace on a one-for-one basis what they expend in resisting the aggression of the Communists who are violating the cease-fire and are fully aided by their Soviet and Red Chinese allies. Congress has already reduced the appropriation to half of what they need and threatens to reduce it even more.

Can we live with ourselves if we, as a nation, betray our friends and ignore our pledged word? And, if we do, who would ever trust us again? To consider committing such an act so contrary to our deepest ideals is symptomatic of the erosion of standards and values. And this adds to our discontent.

We did not seek world leadership; it was thrust upon us. It has been our destiny almost from the first moment this land was settled. If we fail to keep our rendezvous with destiny or, as John Winthrop said in 1630, "Deal falsely with our God," we shall be made "a story and byword throughout the world."

Americans are hungry to feel once again a sense of mission and greatness.

I don 't know about you, but I am impatient with those Republicans who after the last election rushed into print saying, "We must broaden the base of our party" -- when what they meant was to fuzz up and blur even more the differences between ourselves and our opponents.

It was a feeling that there was not a sufficient difference now between the parties that kept a majority of the voters away from the polls. When have we ever advocated a closed-door policy? Who has ever been barred from participating?

Our people look for a cause to believe in. Is it a third party we need, or is it a new and revitalized second party, raising a banner of no pale pastels, but bold colors which make it unmistakably clear where we stand on all of the issues troubling the people?

Let us show that we stand for fiscal integrity and sound money and above all for an end to deficit spending, with ultimate retirement of the national debt.

Let us also include a permanent limit on the percentage of the people's earnings government can take without their consent.

Let our banner proclaim a genuine tax reform that will begin by simplifying the income tax so that workers can compute their obligation without having to employ legal help.

And let it provide indexing -- adjusting the brackets to the cost of living -- so that an increase in salary merely to keep pace with inflation does not move the taxpayer into a surtax bracket. Failure to provide this means an increase in government's share and would make the worker worse off than he was before he got the raise.

Let our banner proclaim our belief in a free market as the greatest provider for the people. Let us also call for an end to the nit-picking, the harassment and over-regulation of business and industry which restricts expansion and our ability to compete in world markets.

Let us explore ways to ward off socialism, not by increasing government's coercive power, but by increasing participation by the people in the ownership of our industrial machine.

Our banner must recognize the responsibility of government to protect the law-abiding, holding those who commit misdeeds personally accountable.

And we must make it plain to international adventurers that our love of peace stops short of "peace at any price."

We will maintain whatever level of strength is necessary to preserve our free way of life.

A political party cannot be all things to all people. It must represent certain fundamental beliefs which must not be compromised to political expediency, or simply to swell its numbers.

I do not believe I have proposed anything that is contrary to what has been considered Republican principle. It is at the same time the very basis of conservatism. It is time to reassert that principle and raise it to full view. And if there are those who cannot subscribe to these principles, then let them go their way.

To Restore America

March 31, 1976

Good evening to all of you from California. Tonight, I'd like to talk to you about issues. Issues which I think are involved--or should be involved in this primary election season. I'm a candidate for the Republican nomination for president. But I hope that you who are Independents and Democrats will let me talk to you also tonight because the problems facing our country are problems that just don't bear any party label.

In this election season the White House is telling us a solid economic recovery is taking place. It claims a slight drop in unemployment. It says that prices aren't going up as fast, but they are still going up, and that the stock market has shown some gains. But, in fact, things seem just about as they were back in the 1972 election year. Remember, we were also coming out of a recession then. Inflation had been running at round 6 percent. Unemployment about 7 [percent]. Remember, too, the upsurge and the optimism lasted through the election year and into 1973. And then the roof fell in. Once again we had unemployment. Only this time not 7 percent, more than 10. And inflation wasn't 6 percent, it was 12 percent. Now, in this election year 1976, we're told we're coming out of this recession just because inflation and unemployment rates have fallen, to what they were at the worst of the previous recession. If history repeats itself, will we be talking recovery four years from now merely because we've reduced inflation from 25 percent to 12 percent?

The fact is, we'll never build a lasting economic recovery by going deeper into debt at a faster rate than we ever have before. It took this nation 166 years until the middle of World War II to finally accumulate a debt of $95 billion. It took this administration just the last 12 months to add $95 billion to the debt. And this administration has run up almost one-fourth of the total national debt in just these short 19 months.

Inflation is the cause of recession and unemployment. And we're not going to have real prosperity or recovery until we stop fighting the symptoms and start fighting the disease. There's only one cause for inflation— government spending more than government takes in. The cure is a balanced budget. Ah, but they tell us, 80 percent of the budget is uncontrollable. It's fixed by laws passed by Congress. Well, laws passed by Congress can be repealed by Congress. And, if Congress is unwilling to do this, then isn't it time we elect a Congress that will?

Soon after he took office, Mr. Ford promised he would end inflation. Indeed, he declared war on inflation. And, we all donned those WIN buttons to "Whip Inflation Now." Unfortunately the war—if it ever really started—was soon over. Mr. Ford without WIN button, appeared on TV, and promised he absolutely would not allow the Federal deficit to exceed $60 billion (which incidentally was $5 billion more than the biggest previous deficit we'd ever had). Later he told us it might be as much as $70 billion. Now we learn it's 80 billion or more.

Then came a White House proposal for a $28 billion tax cut, to be matched by a S28 billion cut in the proposed spending—not in present spending, but in the proposed spending in the new budget.

Well, my question then and my question now is, if there was $28 billion in the new budget that could be cut, what was it doing there in the first place?

Unfortunately, Washington doesn't feel the same pain from inflation that you and I do. As a matter of fact, government makes a profit on inflation. For instance, last July Congress vaccinated itself against that pain. It very quietly passed legislation (which the president signed into law) which automatically now gives a pay increase to every Congressman every time the cost of living goes up.

It would have been nice if they'd thought of some arrangement like that for the rest of us. They could, for example, correct a great unfairness that now exists in our tax system. Today, when you get a cost of living pay raise—one that just keeps you even with purchasing power—it often moves you up into a higher tax bracket. This means you pay a higher percentage in tax, but you reduce your purchasing power. Last year, because of this inequity, the government took in $7 billion in undeserved profit in the income tax alone, and this year they'll do even better.

Now isn't it time that Congress looked after your welfare as well as its own? Those whose spending policies cause inflation to begin with should be made to feel the painful effect just as you and I do.

Repeal of Congress's automatic pay raise might leave it with more incentive to do something to curb inflation. Now, let's look at Social Security. Mr. Ford says he wants to "preserve the integrity of Social Security." Well, I differ with him on one word. I would like to restore the integrity of Social Security. Those who depend on it see a continual reduction in their standard of living. Inflation strips the increase in their benefits. The maximum benefit today buys 80 fewer loaves of bread than it did when that maximum payment was only $85 a month. In the meantime, the Social Security payroll tax has become the most unfair tax any worker pays. Women are discriminated against, particularly working wives. And, people who reach Social Security age and want to continue working, should be allowed to do so without losing their benefits. I believe a presidential commission of experts should be appointed to study and present a plan to strengthen and improve Social Security while there's still time—so that no person who has contributed to Social Security will ever lose a dime.

Before leaving this subject of our economic problems, let's talk about unemployment. Ending inflation is the only long range and lasting answer to the problem of unemployment. The Washington Establishment is not the answer. It's the problem. Its tax policies, its harassing regulation, its confiscation of investment capital to pay for its deficits keeps business and industry from expanding to meet your needs and to provide the jobs we all need.

No one who lived through the Great Depression can ever look upon an unemployed person with anything but compassion. To me, there is no greater tragedy than a breadwinner willing to work, with a job skill but unable to find a market for that job skill. Back in those dark depression days I saw my father on a Christmas eve open what he thought was a Christmas greeting from his boss. Instead, it was the blue slip telling him he no longer had a job. The memory of him sitting there holding that slip of paper and then saying in a half whisper, "That's quite a Christmas present"; it will stay with me as long as I live.

Other problems go unsolved. Take energy. Only a short time ago we were lined up at the gas station— turned our thermostats down as Washington announced "Project Independence." We were going to become self-sufficient, able to provide for our own energy needs. At the time, we were only importing a small percentage of our oil. Yet, the Arab boycott caused half a million Americans to lose their jobs when plants closed down for lack of fuel. Today, it's almost three years later and "Project Independence" has become "Project Dependence." Congress has adopted an energy bill so bad we were led to believe Mr. Ford would veto it. Instead, he signed it. And, almost instantly, drilling rigs all over our land started shutting down. Now, for the first time in our history we are importing more oil than we produce. How many Americans will be laid off if there's another boycott? The energy bill is a disaster that never should have been signed.

An effort has been made in this campaign to suggest that there aren't any real differences between Mr. Ford and myself. Well, I believe there are, and these differences are fundamental. One of them has to do with our approach to government. Before Richard Nixon appointed him Vice President, Mr. Ford was a Congressman for 25 years. His concern, of necessity, was the welfare of his congressional district. For most of his adult life he has been a part of the Washington Establishment. Most of my adult life has been spent outside of government. My experience in government was the eight years I served as governor of California. If it were a nation, California would be the 7th-ranking economic power in the world today.

When I became governor, I inherited a state government that was in almost the same situation as New York City. The state payroll had been growing for a dozen years at a rate of from five to seven thousand new employees each year. State government was spending from a million to a million-and-a-half dollars more each day than it was taking in. The State's great water project was unfinished and under-funded by a half a billion dollars. My predecessor had spent the entire year's budget for Medicaid in the first six months of the fiscal year. And, we learned that the teacher's retirement fund was unfunded—a $4 billion liability hanging over every property owner in the state. I didn't know whether I'd been elected governor or appointed receiver. California was faced with insolvency and on the verge of bankruptcy. We had to increase taxes. Well, this came very hard for me because I felt taxes were already too great a burden. I told the people the increase in my mind was temporary and that, as soon as we could, we'd return their money to them.

I had never in my life thought of seeking or holding public of office and I'm still not quite sure how it all happened. In my own mind, I was a citizen representing my fellow citizens against the institution of government. I turned to the people, not to politicians, for help. Instead of a committee to screen applicants for jobs, I had a citizens' recruiting committee, and I told this committee I wanted an administration made up of men and women who did not want government careers and who'd be the first to tell me if their government job was unnecessary. And I had that happen. [A] young man from the aerospace industry dissolved his department in four months, handed me the key to this office, and told me we'd never needed the department. And to this day, I not only have never missed it—I don't know where it was.

There was a reason for my seeking people who didn't want government careers. Dr. Parkinson summed it all up in his book on bureaucracy. He said, "Government hires a rat-catcher and the first thing you know, he's become a rodent control officer." In those entire eight years, most of us never lost that feeling that we were there representing the people against what Cicero once called the "arrogance of officialdom." We had a kind of watchword we used on each other. "When we begin thinking of government as we instead of they, we've been here too long." Well, I believe that attitude would be beneficial in Washington.

We didn't stop just with getting our administration from the ranks of the people. We also asked for help from expert people in a great many fields, and more than 250 of our citizens volunteered to form into task forces. They went into every department and agency of state government to see how modern business practices could make government more efficient, economical and responsive. They gave an average of 117 days apiece full time, away from their own jobs and careers at no cost to the taxpayers. They made eighteen hundred specific recommendations. We implemented more than sixteen hundred of those recommendations.

This was government-by-the-people, proving that it works when the people work at it. When we ended our eight years, we turned over to the incoming administration a balanced budget, a $500 million surplus, and virtually the same number of employees we'd started with eight years before—even though the increase in population had given some departments a two-thirds increase in work load. The water project was completed with $165 million left over. Our bonds had a triple A rating, the highest credit rating you can get. And the teachers' retirement program was fully funded on a sound actuarial basis. And, we kept our word to the taxpayers—we returned to them in rebates and tax cuts, $5 billion, $761 million.

I believe that what we did in California can be done in Washington if government will have faith in the people and let them bring their common sense to bear on the problems bureaucracy hasn't solved. I believe in the people. Now, Mr. Ford places his faith in the Washington Establishment. This has been evident in his appointment of former Congressmen and longtime government workers to positions in his Administration. Well, I don't believe that those who have been part of the problem are necessarily the best qualified to solve those problems.

The truth is, Washington has taken over functions that don't truly belong to it. In almost every case it has been a failure. Now, understand, I'm speaking of those programs which logically should be administered at state and local levels. Welfare is a classic example. Voices that are raised now and then urging a federalization of welfare don't realize that the failure of welfare is due to federal interference. Washington doesn't even know how many people are on welfare—how many cheaters are getting more than one check. It only knows how many checks it's sending out. Its own rules keep it from finding out how many are getting more than one check.

Well, California had a welfare problem. Sixteen percent of all welfare recipients in the country were drawing their checks in our state. We were sending welfare checks to families who decided to live abroad. One family was receiving its check in Russia. Our caseload was increasing by 40,000 people a month. Well, after a few years of trying to control this runaway program and being frustrated by bureaucrats here in California and in Washington, we turned again to a citizens' task force. The result was the most comprehensive welfare reform ever attempted. And in less than three years we reduced the rolls by more than 300,000 people, saved the taxpayers $2 billion, and increased the grants to the truly deserving needy by an average of 43 percent. We also carried out a successful experiment which I believe is an answer to much of the welfare problem in the nation. We put able-bodied welfare recipients to work at useful community projects in return for their welfare grants.

Now, let's look at housing. Washington has tried to solve this problem for the poor by building low-cost houses. So far it's torn down three and a half homes for every one it's built.

Schools—in America we created at the local level and administered at the local level for many years the greatest public school system in the world. Now through something called federal aid to education, we have something called federal interference, and education has been the loser. Quality has declined as federal intervention has increased. Nothing has created more bitterness, for example, than forced busing to achieve racial balance. It was born of a hope that we could increase understanding and reduce prejudice and antagonism. And I'm sure we all approved of that goal. But busing has failed to achieve the goal. Instead, it has increased the bitterness and animosity it was supposed to reduce. California's Superintendent of Public Instruction, Wilson Riles (himself a Black), says, "The concept that Black children can't learn unless they are sitting with white children is utter and complete nonsense. " Well, I agree. The money now being wasted on this social experiment could be better spent to provide the kind of school facilities every child deserves. Forced busing should be ended by legislation if possible— by constitutional amendment if necessary. And, control of education should be returned to local school districts.

The other day Mr. Ford came out against gun control. But back in Washington, D.C., his Attorney General has proposed a seven-point program that amounts to just that: gun control. I don't think that making it difficult for law-abiding citizens to obtain guns will lower the crime rate— not when the criminals will always find a way to get them. In California I think we found an answer. We put into law what is practical gun control. Anyone convicted of having a gun in his possession while he committed a crime: add five to fifteen years to the prison sentence.

Sometimes bureaucracy's excesses are so great that we laugh at them. But they are costly laughs. Twenty-five years ago the Hoover Commission discovered that Washington files a million reports a year just reporting there is nothing to report. Independent business people, shopkeepers and farmers file billions of reports every year required of them by Washington. It amounts to some 10 billion pieces of paper each year, and it adds $50 billion a year to the cost of doing business. Now, Washington has been loud in its promise to do something about this blizzard of paperwork. And they made good. Last year they increased it by 20 percent.

But there is one problem which must be solved or everything else is meaningless. I am speaking of the problem of our national security. Our nation is in danger, and the danger grows greater with each passing day. Like an echo from the past, the voice of Winston Churchill's grandson was heard recently in Britain's House of Commons warning that the spread of totalitarianism threatens the world once again and the democracies are "wandering without aim."

"Wandering without aim" describes the United States' foreign policy. Angola is a case in point. We gave just enough support to one side to encourage it to fight and die, but too little to give them a chance of winning. And while we're disliked by the winner, distrusted by the loser, and viewed by the world as weak and unsure. If détente were the two-way street it's supposed to be, we could have told the Soviet Union to stop its trouble-making and leave Angola to the Angolans. But it didn't work out that way.

Now, we are told Washington is dropping the word "détente," but keeping the policy. But whatever it's called, the policy is what's at fault. What is our policy? Mr. Ford's new Ambassador to the United Nations attacks our longtime ally, Israel. In Asia, our new relationship with mainland China can have practical benefits for both sides. But that doesn't mean it should include yielding to demands by them, as the administration has, to reduce our military presence on Taiwan where we have a longtime friend and ally, the Republic of China.

And, it's also revealed now that we seek to establish friendly relations with Hanoi. To make it more palatable, we're told that this might help us learn the fate of the men still listed as Missing in Action. Well, there's no doubt our government has an obligation to end the agony of parents, wives and children who've lived so long with uncertainty. But, this should have been one of our first demands of Hanoi's patron saint, the Soviet Union, if détente had any meaning at all. To present it now as a reason for friendship with those who have already violated their promise to provide such information is hypocrisy.

In the last few days, Mr. Ford and Dr. Kissinger have taken us from hinting at invasion of Cuba, to laughing it off as a ridiculous idea. Except, that it was their ridiculous idea. No one else suggested it. Once again— what is their policy? During this last year, they carried on a campaign to befriend Castro. They persuaded the Organization of American States to lift its trade embargo, lifted some of the U.S. trade restrictions. They engaged in cultural exchanges. And then, on the eve of the Florida primary election, Mr. Ford went to Florida, called Castro an outlaw and said he'd never recognize him. But he hasn't asked our Latin American neighbors to reimpose a single sanction, nor has he taken any action himself. Meanwhile, Castro continues to export revolution to Puerto Rico, to Angola, and who knows where else?

As I talk to you tonight, negotiations with another dictator go forward— negotiations aimed at giving up our ownership of the Panama Canal Zone. Apparently, everyone knows about this except the rightful owners of the Canal Zone—you, the people of the United States. General Omar Torrijos, the dictator of Panama, seized power eight years ago by ousting the duly-elected government. There have been no elections since. No civil liberties. The press is censored. Torrijos is a friend and ally of Castro and, like him, is pro-Communist. He threatens sabotage and guerrilla attacks on our installations if we don't yield to his demands. His foreign minister openly claims that we have already agreed in principle to giving up the Canal Zone.

Well, the Canal Zone is not a colonial possession. It is not a long-term lease. It is sovereign United States Territory every bit the same as Alaska and all the states that were carved from the Louisiana Purchase. We should end those negotiations and tell the General: We bought it, we paid for it, we built it, and we intend to keep it.

Mr. Ford says détente will be replaced by "peace through strength." Well now, that slogan has a—a nice ring to it, but neither Mr. Ford nor his new Secretary of Defense will say that our strength is superior to all others. In one of the dark hours of the Great Depression, Franklin Delano Roosevelt said, "It is time to speak the truth frankly and boldly." Well, I believe former Secretary of Defense James Schlesinger was trying to speak the truth frankly and boldly to his fellow citizens. And that's why he is no longer Secretary of Defense.

The Soviet Army outnumbers ours more than two-to-one and in reserves four-to-one. They out-spend us on weapons by 50 percent. Their Navy outnumbers ours in surface ships and submarines two-to-one. We're outgunned in artillery three-to-one and their tanks outnumber ours four-to-one. Their strategic nuclear missiles are larger, more powerful and more numerous than ours. The evidence mounts that we are Number Two in a world where it's dangerous, if not fatal, to be second best. Is this why Mr. Ford refused to invite Alexander Solzhenitsyn to the White House? Or, why Mr. Ford traveled halfway 'round the world to sign the Helsinki Pact, putting our stamp of approval on Russia's enslavement of the captive nations? We gave away the freedom of millions of people— freedom that was not ours to give.

Now we must ask if someone is giving away our own freedom. Dr. Kissinger is quoted as saying that he thinks of the United States as Athens and the Soviet Union as Sparta. "The day of the U.S. is past and today is the day of the Soviet Union." And he added, ". . . My job as Secretary of State is to negotiate the most acceptable second-best position available." Well, I believe in the peace of which Mr. Ford spoke—as much as any man. But peace does not come from weakness or from retreat. It comes from the restoration of American military superiority.

Ask the people of Latvia, Estonia, Lithuania, Czechoslovakia, Poland, Hungary—all the others: East Germany, Bulgaria, Romania—ask them what it's like to live in a world where the Soviet Union is Number One. I don't want to live in that kind of world; and I don't think you do either. Now we learn that another high official of the State Department, Helmut Sonnenfeldt, whom Dr. Kissinger refers to as his "Kissinger," has expressed the belief that, in effect, the captive nations should give up any claim of national sovereignty and simply become a part of the Soviet Union. He says, "their desire to break out of the Soviet straightjacket" threatens us with World War III. In other words, slaves should accept their fate.

Well, I don't believe the people I've met in almost every State of this Union are ready to consign this, the last island of freedom, to the dust bin of history, along with the bones of dead civilizations of the past. Call it mysticism, if you will, but I believe God had a divine purpose in placing this land between the two great oceans to be found by those who had a special love of freedom and the courage to leave the countries of their birth. From our forefathers to our modern-day immigrants, we've come from every corner of the earth, from every race and every ethnic background, and we've become a new breed in the world. We're Americans and we have a rendezvous with destiny. We spread across this land, building farms and towns and cities, and we did it without any federal land planning program or urban renewal.

Indeed, we gave birth to an entirely new concept in man's relation to man. We created government as our servant, beholden to us and possessing no powers except those voluntarily granted to it by us. Now a self-anointed elite in our nation's capital would have us believe we are incapable of guiding our own destiny. They practice government by mystery, telling us it's too complex for our understanding. Believing this, they assume we might panic if we were to be told the truth about our problems.

Why should we become frightened? No people who have ever lived on this earth have fought harder, paid a higher price for freedom, or done more to advance the dignity of man than the living Americans—the Americans living in this land today. There isn't any problem we can't solve if government will give us the facts. Tell us what needs to be done. Then, get out of the way and let us have at it.

Recently on one of my campaign trips I was doing a question-and-answer session, and suddenly I received a question from a little girl—couldn't have been over six or seven years old—standing in the very front row. I'd heard the question before but somehow in her asking it, she threw me a little bit. She said, why do you want to be president? Well, I tried to tell her about giving government back to the people; I tried to tell her about turning authority back to the states and local communities, and so forth; winding down the bureaucracy. [It] might have been an answer for adults, but I knew that it wasn't what that little girl wanted, and I left very frustrated. It was on the way to the next stop that I turned to Nancy and I said I wish I had it to do over again because I—I'd like to answer her question.

Well, maybe I can answer it now. I would like to go to Washington. I would like to be president, because I would like to see this country become once again a country where a little six-year old girl can grow up knowing the same freedom that I knew when I was six years old, growing up in America. If this is the America you want for yourself and your children; if you want to restore government not only of and for but by the people; to see the American spirit unleashed once again; to make this land a shining, golden hope God intended it to be, I'd like to hear from you. Write, or send a wire. I'd be proud to hear your thoughts and your ideas.

Thank you, and good night.

The New Republican Party

February 6, 1977
4th Annual CPAC Convention

I'm happy to be back with you in this annual event after missing last year's meeting. I had some business in New Hampshire that wouldn't wait.

Three weeks ago here in our nation's capital I told a group of conservative scholars that we are currently in the midst of a re-ordering of the political realities that have shaped our time. We know today that the principles and values that lie at the heart of conservatism are shared by the majority.

Despite what some in the press may say, we who are proud to call ourselves "conservative" are not a minority of a minority party; we are part of the great majority of Americans of both major parties and of most of the independents as well.

A Harris poll released September 7, 1975 showed 18 percent identifying themselves as liberal and 31 percent as conservative, with 41 percent as middle of the road; a few months later, on January 5, 1976, by a 43-19 plurality, those polled by Harris said they would "prefer to see the country move in a more conservative direction than a liberal one."

Last October 24th, the Gallup organization released the result of a poll taken right in the midst of the presidential campaign.

Respondents were asked to state where they would place themselves on a scale ranging from "right-of-center" (which was defined as "conservative") to left-of-center (which was defined as "liberal").

* Thirty-seven percent viewed themselves as left-of-center or liberal * Twelve percent placed themselves in the middle * Fifty-one percent said they were right-of-center, that is, conservative.

What I find interesting about this particular poll is that it offered those polled a range of choices on a left-right continuum. This seems to me to be a more realistic approach than dividing the world into strict left and rights. Most of us, I guess, like to think of ourselves as avoiding both extremes, and the fact that a majority of Americans chose one or the other position on the right end of the spectrum is really impressive.

Those polls confirm that most Americans are basically conservative in their outlook. But once we have said this, we conservatives have not solved our problems, we have merely stated them clearly. Yes, conservatism can and does mean different things to those who call themselves conservatives.

You know, as I do, that most commentators make a distinction between [what] they call "social" conservatism and "economic" conservatism. The so-called social issues -- law and order, abortion, busing, quota systems -- are usually associated with blue-collar, ethnic and religious groups themselves traditionally associated with the Democratic Party. The economic issues -- inflation, deficit spending and big government -- are usually associated with Republican Party members and independents who concentrate their attention on economic matters.

Now I am willing to accept this view of two major kinds of conservatism -- or, better still, two different conservative constituencies. But at the same time let me say that the old lines that once clearly divided these two kinds of conservatism are disappearing.

In fact, the time has come to see if it is possible to present a program of action based on political principle that can attract those interested in the so-called "social" issues and those interested in "economic" issues. In short, isn't it possible to combine the two major segments of contemporary American conservatism into one politically effective whole?

I believe the answer is: Yes, it is possible to create a political entity that will reflect the views of the great, hitherto [unacknowledged], conservative majority. We went a long way toward doing it in California. We can do it in America. This is not a dream, a wistful hope. It is and has been a reality. I have seen the conservative future and it works.

Let me say again what I said to our conservative friends from the academic world: What I envision is not simply a melding together of the two branches of American conservatism into a temporary uneasy alliance, but the creation of a new, lasting majority.

This will mean compromise. But not a compromise of basic principle. What will emerge will be something new: something open and vital and dynamic, something the great conservative majority will recognize as its own, because at the heart of this undertaking is principled politics.

I have always been puzzled by the inability of some political and media types to understand exactly what is meant by adherence to political principle. All too often in the press and the television evening news it is treated as a call for "ideological purity." Whatever ideology may mean -- and it seems to mean a variety of things, depending upon who is using it -- it always conjures up in my mind a picture of a rigid, irrational clinging to abstract theory in the face of reality. We have to recognize that in this country "ideology" is a scare word. And for good reason. Marxist-Leninism is, to give but one example, an ideology. All the facts of the real world have to be fitted to the Procrustean bed of Marx and Lenin. If the facts don't happen to fit the ideology, the facts are chopped off and discarded.

I consider this to be the complete opposite to principled conservatism. If there is any political viewpoint in this world which is free from slavish adherence to abstraction, it is American conservatism.

When a conservative states that the free market is the best mechanism ever devised by the mind of man to meet material needs, he is merely stating what a careful examination of the real world has told him is the truth.

When a conservative says that totalitarian Communism is an absolute enemy of human freedom he is not theorizing -- he is reporting the ugly reality captured so unforgettably in the writings of Alexander Solzhenitsyn.

When a conservative says it is bad for the government to spend more than it takes in, he is simply showing the same common sense that tells him to come in out of the rain.

When a conservative says that busing does not work, he is not appealing to some theory of education -- he is merely reporting what he has seen down at the local school.

When a conservative quotes Jefferson that government that is closest to the people is best, it is because he knows that Jefferson risked his life, his fortune and his sacred honor to make certain that what he and his fellow patriots learned from experience was not crushed by an ideology of empire.

Conservatism is the antithesis of the kind of ideological fanaticism that has brought so much horror and destruction to the world. The common sense and common decency of ordinary men and women, working out their own lives in their own way -- this is the heart of American conservatism today. Conservative wisdom and principles are derived from willingness to learn, not just from what is going on now, but from what has happened before.

The principles of conservatism are sound because they are based on what men and women have discovered through experience in not just one generation or a dozen, but in all the combined experience of mankind. When we conservatives say that we know something about political affairs, and that we know can be stated as principles, we are saying that the principles we hold dear are those that have been found, through experience, to be ultimately beneficial for individuals, for families, for communities and for nations -- found through the often bitter testing of pain, or sacrifice and sorrow.

One thing that must be made clear in post-Watergate is this: The American new conservative majority we represent is not based on abstract theorizing of the kind that turns off the American people, but on common sense, intelligence, reason, hard work, faith in God, and the guts to say: "Yes, there are things we do strongly believe in, that we are willing to live for, and yes, if necessary, to die for." That is not "ideological purity." It is simply what built this country and kept it great.

Let us lay to rest, once and for all, the myth of a small group of ideological purists trying to capture a majority. Replace it with the reality of a majority trying to assert its rights against the tyranny of powerful academics, fashionable left-revolutionaries, some economic illiterates who happen to hold elective office and the social engineers who dominate the dialogue and set the format in political and social affairs. If there is any ideological fanaticism in American political life, it is to be found among the enemies of freedom on the left or right -- those who would sacrifice principle to theory, those who worship only the god of political, social and economic abstractions, ignoring the realities of everyday life. They are not conservatives.

Our first job is to get this message across to those who share most of our principles. If we allow ourselves to be portrayed as ideological shock troops without correcting this error we are doing ourselves and our cause a disservice. Wherever and whenever we can, we should gently but firmly correct our political and media friends who have been perpetuating the myth of conservatism as a narrow ideology. Whatever the word may have meant in the past, today conservatism means principles evolving from experience and a belief in change when necessary, but not just for the sake of change.

Once we have established this, the next question is: What will be the political vehicle by which the majority can assert its rights?

I have to say I cannot agree with some of my friends -- perhaps including some of you here tonight -- who have answered that question by saying this nation needs a new political party.

I respect that view and I know that those who have reached it have done so after long hours of study. But I believe that political success of the principles we believe in can best be achieved in the Republican Party. I believe the Republican Party can hold and should provide the political mechanism through which the goals of the majority of Americans can be achieved. For one thing, the biggest single grouping of conservatives is to be found in that party. It makes more sense to build on that grouping than to break it up and start over. Rather than a third party, we can have a new first party made up of people who share our principles. I have said before that if a formal change in name proves desirable, then so be it. But tonight, for purpose of discussion, I'm going to refer to it simply as the New Republican Party.

And let me say so there can be no mistakes as to what I mean: The New Republican Party I envision will not be, and cannot, be one limited to the country club-big business image that, for reasons both fair and unfair, it is burdened with today. The New Republican Party I am speaking about is going to have room for the man and the woman in the factories, for the farmer, for the cop on the beat and the millions of Americans who may never have thought of joining our party before, but whose interests coincide with those represented by principled Republicanism. If we are to attract more working men and women of this country, we will do so not by simply "making room" for them, but by making certain they have a say in what goes on in the party. The Democratic Party turned its back on the majority of social conservatives during the 1960s. The

New Republican Party of the late '70s and '80s must welcome them, seek them out, enlist them, not only as rank-and-file members but as leaders and as candidates.

The time has come for Republicans to say to black voters: "Look, we offer principles that black Americans can, and do, support." We believe in jobs, real jobs; we believe in education that is really education; we believe in treating all Americans as individuals and not as stereotypes or voting blocs -- and we believe that the long-range interest of black Americans lies in looking at what each major party has to offer, and then deciding on the merits. The Democratic Party takes the black vote for granted. Well, it's time black America and the New Republican Party move toward each other and create a situation in which no black vote can be taken for granted.

The New Republican Party I envision is one that will energetically seek out the best candidates for every elective office, candidates who not only agree with, but understand, and are willing to fight for a sound, honest economy, for the interests of American families and neighborhoods and communities and a strong national defense. And these candidates must be able to communicate those principles to the American people in language they understand. Inflation isn't a textbook problem. Unemployment isn't a textbook problem. They should be discussed in human terms.

Our candidates must be willing to communicate with every level of society, because the principles we espouse are universal and cut across traditional lines. In every Congressional district there should be a search made for young men and women who share these principles and they should be brought into positions of leadership in the local Republican Party groups. We can find attractive, articulate candidates if we look, and when we find them, we will begin to change the sorry state of affairs that has led to a Democratic-controlled Congress for more than 40 years. I need not remind you that you can have the soundest principles in the world, but if you don't have candidates who can communicate those principles, candidates who are articulate as well as principled, you are going to lose election after election. I refuse to believe that the good Lord divided this world into Republicans who defend basic values and Democrats who win elections. We have to find tough, bright young men and women who are sick and tired of cliches and the pomposity and the mind-numbing economic idiocy of the liberals in Washington.

It is at this point, however, that we come across a question that is really the essential one: What will be the basis of this New Republican Party? To what set of values and principles can our candidates appeal? Where can Americans who want to know where we stand look for guidance?

Fortunately, we have an answer to that question. That answer was provided last summer by the men and women of the Republican Party -- not just the leadership, but the ones who have built the party on local levels all across the country.

The answer was provided in the 1976 platform of the Republican Party.

This was not a document handed down from on high. It was hammered out in free and open debate among all those who care about our party and the principles it stands for.

The Republican platform is unique. Unlike any other party platform I have ever seen, it answers not only programmatic questions for the immediate future of the party but also provides a clear outline of the underlying principles upon which those programs are based.

The New Republican Party can and should use the Republican platform of 1976 as the major source from which a Declaration of Principles can be created and offered to the American people.

Tonight I want to offer to you my own version of what such a declaration might look like. I make no claim to originality. This declaration I propose is relatively short, taken, for most part, word for word from the Republican platform. It concerns itself with basic principles, not with specific solutions.

We, the members of the New Republican Party, believe that the preservation and enhancement of the values that strengthen and protect individual freedom, family life, communities and neighborhoods and the liberty of our beloved nation should be at the heart of any legislative or political program presented to the American people. Toward that end, we, therefore, commit ourselves to the following propositions and offer them to each American believing that the New Republican Party, based on such principles, will serve the interest of all the American people.

We believe that liberty can be measured by how much freedom Americans have to make their own decisions, even their own mistakes. Government must step in when one's liberties impinge on one's neighbor's. Government must protect constitutional rights, deal with other governments, protect citizens from aggressors, assure equal opportunity, and be compassionate in caring for those citizens who are unable to care for themselves.

Our federal system of local-state-national government is designed to sort out on what level these actions should be taken. Those concerns of a national character -- such as air and water pollution that do not respect state boundaries, or the national transportation system, or efforts to safeguard your civil liberties -- must, of course, be handled on the national level.

As a general rule, however, we believe that government action should be taken first by the government that resides as close to you as possible.

We also believe that Americans, often acting through voluntary organizations, should have the opportunity to solve many of the social problems of their communities. This spirit of freely helping others is uniquely American and should be encouraged in every way by government.

Families must continue to be the foundation of our nation.

Families -- not government programs -- are the best way to make sure our children are properly nurtured, our elderly are cared for, our cultural and spiritual heritages are perpetuated, our laws are observed and our values are preserved.

Thus it is imperative that our government's programs, actions, officials and social welfare institutions never be allowed to jeopardize the family. We fear the government may be powerful enough to destroy our families; we know that it is not powerful enough to replace them. The New Republican Party must be committed to working always in the interest of the American family.

Every dollar spent by government is a dollar earned by individuals. Government must always ask: Are your dollars being wisely spent?

Can we afford it? Is it not better for the country to leave your dollars in your pocket?

Elected officials, their appointees, and government workers are expected to perform their public acts with honesty, openness, diligence, and special integrity.

Government must work for the goal of justice and the elimination of unfair practices, but no government has yet designed a more productive economic system or one which benefits as many people as the American market system.

The beauty of our land is our legacy to our children. It must be protected by us so that they can pass it on intact to their children.

The United States must always stand for peace and liberty in the world and the rights of the individual. We must form sturdy partnerships with our allies for the preservation of freedom. We must be ever willing to negotiate differences, but equally mindful that there are American ideals that cannot be compromised. Given that there are other nations with potentially hostile design, we recognize that we can reach our goals only while maintaining a superior national defense, second to none.

In his inaugural speech President Carter said that he saw the world "dominated by a new spirit." He said, and I quote: "The passion for freedom is on the rise."

Well, I don't know how he knows this, but if it is true, then it is the most unrequited passion in human history. The world is being dominated by a new spirit, all right, but it isn't the spirit of freedom.

It isn't very often you see a familiar object that shocks and frightens you. But the other day I came across a map of the world created by Freedom House, an organization monitoring the state of freedom in the world for the past 25 years. It is an ordinary map, with one exception: it shows the world's nations in white for free, shaded for partly free and black for not free.

Almost all of the great Eurasian land mass is completely colored black, from the western border of East Germany, through middle and eastern Europe, through the awesome spaces of the Soviet Union, on to the Bering Strait in the north, down past the immensity of China, still further down to Vietnam and the South China Sea -- in all that huge, sprawling, inconceivably immense area not a single political or personal or religious freedom exists. The entire continent of Africa, from the Mediterranean to the Cape of Good Hope, from the Atlantic to the Indian Ocean, all that vastness is almost totally unfree. In the tiny nation of Tanzania alone, according to a report in the New York Times, there are 3,000 people in detention for political crimes -- that is more than the total being held in South Africa! The Mideast has only one free state: Israel. If a visitor from another planet were to approach earth, and if this planet showed free nations in light and unfree nations in darkness, the pitifully small beacons of light would make him wonder what was hidden in that terrifying, enormous blackness.

We know what is hidden: Gulag. Torture. Families -- and human beings -- broken apart. No free press, no freedom of religion. The ancient forms of tyranny revived and made even more hideous and strong through what Winston Churchill once called "a perverted science." Men rotting for years in solitary confinement because they have different political and economic beliefs, solitary confinement that drives the fortunate ones insane and makes the survivors wish for death.

Only now and then do we in the West hear a voice from out of that darkness. Then there is silence -- the silence of human slavery. There is no more terrifying sound in human experience, with one possible exception. Look at that map again. The very heart of the darkness is the Soviet Union and from that heart comes a different sound. It is the whirring sound of machinery and the whisper of the computer technology we ourselves have sold them. It is the sound of building, building of the strongest military machine ever devised by man. Our military strategy is designed to hopefully prevent a war. Theirs is designed to win one. A group of eminent scientists, scholars and intelligence experts offer a survey showing that the Soviet Union is driving for military superiority and are derided as hysterically making, quote, "a worst case," unquote, concerning Soviet intentions and capabilities.

But is it not precisely the duty of the national government to be prepared for the worst case? Two Senators, after studying the North Atlantic Treaty Organization, have reported to the Armed Forces Committee that Soviet forces in Eastern Europe have the capability to launch, with little warning, a "potentially devastating" attack in Central Europe from what is termed a "standing alert."

Reading their report, one can almost see the enormous weight of the parts of the earth that are under tyranny shifting in an irresistible tilt toward that tiny portion of land in freedom's light. Even now in Western Europe we have Communists in the government of Italy, France appeasing terrorists, and England -- for centuries the model or the sword of freedom in Western Europe -- weak, dispirited, turning inward.

A "worst case"? How could you make a good case out of the facts as they are known? The Soviet Union, poised on the edge of free Europe, capable of striking from a standing start, has modern tanks in far greater numbers than the outmoded vehicles of NATO. We have taken comfort from NATO's superiority in the air, but now the Soviet Union has made a dramatic swing away from its historic defensive air posture to one capable of supporting offensive action. NATO's southern flank is described in the Senate report with a single word: shambles.

The report is simply reality as it was, with different names and faces, in Europe in the late 1930s when so many refused to believe and thought if we don't look the threat will go away.

We don't want hysteria. We don't want distortion of Soviet power. We want truth. And above all we want peace. And to have [recognition] that the United States has to immediately re-examine its entire view of the world and develop a strategy of freedom. We cannot be the second-best super-power for the simple reason that he who is second is last. In this deadly game, there are no silver medals for second.

President Carter, as a candidate, said he would cut five to seven billion dollars from the defense budget. We must let him know that while we agree, there must be no fat in our armed forces. Those armed forces must be capable of coping with the new reality presented to us by the Russians, and cutting seven billion dollars out of our defense budget is not the way to accomplish this. Some years ago, a young President said, we will make any sacrifice, bear any burden, and we will, to preserve our freedom.

Our relationship with mainland China is clouded. The so-called "Gang of Four" are up one day and down the next and we are seeing the pitfalls of making deals with charismatic personalities and living legends. The charisma fades as the living legends die, and those who take their place are interested not in our best wishes but in power. The keyword for China today is turmoil. We should watch and observe and analyze as closely and rationally as we can.

But in our relationships with the mainland of China we should always remember that the conditions and possibilities for and the realities of freedom exist to an infinitely greater degree with our Chinese friends in Taiwan. We can never go wrong if we do what is morally right, and the moral way -- the honorable way -- is to keep our commitment, our solemn promise to the people of Taiwan. Our liberal friends have made much of the lack of freedom in some Latin American countries. Senator Edward Kennedy and his colleagues here in Washington let no opportunity pass to let us know about horrors in Chile.

Well, I think when the United States of America is considering a deal with a country that hasn't had an election in almost eight years, where the press is under the thumb of a dictatorship, where ordinary citizens are abducted in the night by secret police, where military domination of the country is known to be harsh on dissenters and when these things are documented, we should reject overtures from those who rule such a country.

But the country I'm describing is not Chile -- it is Panama.

We are negotiating with a dictatorship that comes within the portion of that map colored black for no freedom. No civil rights. One-man rule. No free press.

Candidate Carter said he would never relinquish "actual control" of the Panama Canal. President Carter is negotiating with a dictatorship whose record on civil and human rights is as I have just described and the negotiations concern the rights guaranteed to us by treaty which we will give up under a threat of violence. In only a few weeks we will mark the second anniversary of the death of freedom for the Vietnamese. An estimated 300,000 of them are being "re-educated" in concentration camps to forget about freedom.

There is only one major question on the agenda of national priorities and that is the state of our national security. I refer, of course, to the state of our armed forces -- but also to our state of mind, to the way we perceive the world. We cannot maintain the strength we need to survive, no matter how many missiles we have, no matter how many tanks we build, unless we are willing to reverse:

* The trend of deteriorating faith in and continuing abuse of our national intelligence agencies. Let's stop the sniping and the propaganda and the historical revisionism and let the CIA and the other intelligence agencies do their job!

* Let us reverse the trend of public indifference to problems of national security. In every congressional district citizens should join together, enlist and educate neighbors and make certain that congressmen know we care. The front pages of major newspapers on the East Coast recently headlined and told in great detail of a

takeover, the takeover of a magazine published in New York -- not a nation losing its freedom. You would think, from the attention it received in the media, that it was a matter of blazing national interest whether the magazine lived or died. The tendency of much of the media to ignore the state of our national security is too well documented for me to go on.

My friends, the time has come to start acting to bring about the great conservative majority party we know is waiting to be created.

And just to set the record straight, let me say this about our friends who are now Republicans but who do not identify themselves as conservatives: I want the record to show that I do not view the new revitalized Republican Party as one based on a principle of exclusion. After all, you do not get to be a majority party by searching for groups you won't associate or work with. If we truly believe in our principles, we should sit down and talk. Talk with anyone, anywhere, at any time if it means talking about the principles for the Republican Party. Conservatism is not a narrow ideology, nor is it the exclusive property of conservative activists.

We've succeeded better than we know. Little more than a decade ago more than two-thirds of Americans believed the federal government could solve all our problems, and do so without restricting our freedom or bankrupting the nation.

We warned of things to come, of the danger inherent in unwarranted government involvement in things not its proper province. What we warned against has come to pass. And today more than two-thirds of our citizens are telling us, and each other, that social engineering by the federal government has failed. The Great Society is great only in power, in size and in cost. And so are the problems it set out to solve. Freedom has been diminished and we stand on the brink of economic ruin.

Our task now is not to sell a philosophy, but to make the majority of Americans, who already share that philosophy, see that modern conservatism offers them a political home. We are not a cult, we are members of a majority. Let's act and talk like it.

The job is ours and the job must be done. If not by us, who? If not now, when?

Our party must be the party of the individual. It must not sell out the individual to cater to the group. No greater challenge faces our society today than ensuring that each one of us can maintain his dignity and his identity in an increasingly complex, centralized society.

Extreme taxation, excessive controls, oppressive government competition with business, galloping inflation, frustrated minorities and forgotten Americans are not the products of free enterprise. They are the residue of centralized bureaucracy, of government by a self-anointed elite.

Our party must be based on the kind of leadership that grows and takes its strength from the people. Any organization is in actuality only the lengthened shadow of its members. A political party is a mechanical structure created to further a cause. The cause, not the mechanism, brings and holds the members together. And our cause must be to rediscover, reassert and reapply America's spiritual heritage to our national affairs.

Then with God's help we shall indeed be as a city upon a hill with the eyes of all people upon us.

America's Purpose in the World

March 17, 1978
5th Annual CPAC Conference

As a part-time journalist faced with producing a syndicated daily radio broadcast and twice-a-week newspaper column, I find being on the mailing lists of an almost endless array of organizations most helpful. Now some of the flood of materials crosses my desk very swiftly. But not all of it. One thick handout I got late last year was especially fascinating, not only because of content but just because it was mailed to me at all.

It was from the White House Press Office. Under the title "Domestic and Foreign Policy Accomplishments" it told me, in 21 single-spaced pages, of the wonders of the Carter administration's first year.

Beginning with the modest statement that - quote - "The president tackled directly and comprehensively major domestic problems that had been almost completely ignored in previous years." - unquote - it then recited an impressive list of major accomplishments. True, the White House hadn't claimed to find a way to control the weather or to eliminate crab grass on the White House lawn, but it did think it had solved -- or nearly solved -- our energy problems, Social Security's $17-trillion deficit, the size of a big government (we added 52,000 new employees in the first 10 months of 1977), the welfare mess and a host of other problems that have been center stage in American life for quite some time.

Tonight, perhaps we should discuss some of those White House claims and see if they have stood the test of even the three months

that have passed since they were made. I know that's a little cruel --
like checking up on someone's New Year's resolutions. After all, the
administration has scarcely gotten a single domestic program worth
noting through Congress. I'll tell you what. Let us concentrate on
the administration's handling of foreign affairs, national security
and its sense of priorities.

On priorities, there is the matter of issuing the former budget
director a diplomatic passport; the taking of depositions from
bartenders and issuing a 33-page denial that the president's chief
aide expectorated at or in the direction of a young woman. It
boggles the mind to think what they would have done if he'd spit on
the sidewalk. Then there was the solemn oath to appoint and retain
a U.S. attorney who goes investigating suspected wrongdoing on
the part of Congressmen who belong to the president's own party.

Moving on to the Carter administration's record in foreign affairs --
let me say a few words about Panama and our canal there. And I do
mean a few words.

With yesterday's vote on the so-called Neutrality Treaty, you might
say that round one is over. Now, there has been confusion in some
news reports which called this the "first treaty," saying that the
Senate would next take up the "second treaty." Actually, the Senate
decided to reverse the procedure. The Neutrality Treaty is the
second treaty. They just voted on it first. Next they will deal with
the basic treaty, the one called the Panama Canal Treaty. It is the
basic treaty because it is the one which would relinquish our rights
and would actually eliminate the canal zone as soon as it goes into
effect -- if it does.

I hope the Senate will devote as much detailed attention to this basic treaty as it did to the Neutrality Treaty. Meanwhile, I can't get a question out of my head. It is this: Even though the Neutrality Treaty supposedly guarantees our right to go back in to defend the Canal after 1999, if there is no canal zone, wouldn't any such move on out part be branded as interference in the internal affairs of Panama?

On the other hand, if the basic treaty is not ratified, the Neutrality Treaty itself won't have much meaning because our rights and our presence in the canal zone would continue. And, when all is said and done, it is always easier to defend something you have than to get back something you gave away.

My fundamental concern has always been primarily with this basic treaty which would eliminate our rights there. I think there are alternatives to it which would be better for all concerned.

You are all activists, and I know you will make your views known to your elected representatives on this next treaty debate.

My purpose tonight, however, is not to repeat my views on this question. Panama is an important issue. The final outcome is not yet certain, and certainly the matter won't end with the final vote in the Senate. In a way, that will only begin it.

But, whatever the outcome on Capitol Hill, the smug assumptions of many of the treaties' proponents have been successfully and vigorously challenged.

Few Americans accept the belief of some of those now in positions of importance in guiding our foreign policy that America's purpose in the world is to appease the mighty out of a sense of fear or to appease the weak out of a sense of guilt.

But a question remains. Is the faulty thinking that has led us to these particular treaties an isolated particle, or is it part of a much larger whole?

In reviewing the foreign policy of this administration, one can only come to the conclusion that the mistaken assumptions that led to its course on the Panama Canal treaties are being duplicated around the world.

Its policy is rooted in well-meaning intentions, but it shows a woeful uncertainty as to America's purpose in the world.

The administration means to do good by espousing a human rights doctrine it cannot define, much less implement. In the process, this policy has met with scorn from our enemies and alarm from our friends. That self-graded, 21-page White House report card said, with regard to human rights, "The president has strengthened our human rights policy and we are letting it be known clearly that the United States stands with the victims of repression." Is that why our representatives at the Belgrade Conference remained silent in the face of a final report that contained not one word about Russian violations of the human rights provisions in the Helsinki Agreement?

If the Carter administration "stands with the victims of repression," the people of Cuba, Panama, Vietnam, Cambodia, and the mainland of China have yet to hear about it. The fact is, the Carter human rights policy is whatever his appointees who guide it want it to be. In practice, they have ceaselessly scolded authoritarian governments of countries that are friendly and ignored authoritarian and totalitarian countries that are not.

Mr. Carter might find a reading of the historian Charles Beard informative. Nearly 40 years ago, Beard concluded that the defect of a foreign policy based on what he called "the selfish sacrifice required by an absolute morality" was the inability to understand "the limited nature of American powers to relieve, restore and maintain life beyond its own sphere of interest and control - a recognition of the hard fact that the United States ... did not possess the power ... to assure the establishment of democratic and pacific government."

But, by using a combination of heavy-handed moves against allied countries, on the one hand, and making "pre-emptive concessions" toward unfriendly or potentially unfriendly countries on the other, the Carter administration has managed to convey the view that it desperately wants the whole world to have democratic institutions that would be the envy of the most ardent ACLU lawyer, and that wishing will make it so.

That view of the world ranks along with belief in the Tooth Fairy. But confusion of purpose and a false sense of guilt are not the only elements in this administration's foreign policy.

Too often, the president is advised by men and women who are forever trapped in the tragic but still fresh memory of a lost war. And from Vietnam they have drawn all the wrong lessons. When they say "never again," they mean the United States should never again resist Communist aggression.

In saying "never again," implying that the war should have been lost -- that it is all right for the victors to conduct a brutal campaign against their own people, violating even minimal human rights.

That it is alright to ignore these massive violations and alright for us to seek better relations with the governments responsible. That White House document lists as an "accomplishment" the fact that "the administration has started the process of normalizing relations" with the Communist conquerors of South Vietnam. The lesson we should have learned from Vietnam is that never again will Americans be asked to fight and die unless they are permitted to win. We need a foreign policy stripped of platitudes, cant and mere moral earnestness -- an earnestness fatally compromised by the massive crimes of some of the Communist world's newer members.

This pattern of Communist violations of human rights should come as no surprise to us. Over and over again, newly established Marxist regimes have committed them. In the 1920s and '30s it was the Soviet Union, in the late '40s the new Iron Curtain countries, in the '50s and through the Cultural Revolution of the '60s it was Communist China and Cuba, and now it is Vietnam and Cambodia.

The problem with much of the Carter team is that they know too little, not too much, of history. And, they have lost faith in their own country's past and traditions.

Too often, that team has operated under the assumption that the United States must prove and reprove and prove again its goodness to the world. Proving that we are civilized in a world that is often uncivilized -- and unapologetically so -- is hardly necessary.

The themes of a sound foreign policy should be no mystery, nor the result of endless agonizing reappraisals. They are rooted in our past -- in our very beginning as a nation.

The Founding Fathers established a system which meant a radical break from that which preceded it. A written constitution would provide a permanent form of government, limited in scope, but effective in providing both liberty and order. Government was not to be a matter of self-appointed rulers, governing by whim or harsh ideology. It was not to be government by the strongest or for the few. Our principles were revolutionary. We began as a small, weak republic. But we survived. Our example inspired others, imperfectly at times, but it inspired them nevertheless. This constitutional republic, conceived in liberty and dedicated to the proposition that all men are created equal, prospered and grew strong. To this day, America is still the abiding alternative to tyranny. That is our purpose in the world -- nothing more and nothing less.

To carry out that purpose, our fundamental aim in foreign policy must be to ensure our own survival and to protect those others who share our values. Under no circumstances should we have any illusions about the intentions of those who are enemies of freedom. Our Communist adversaries have little regard for human rights because they have little interest in human freedom. The ruling elites of those countries wish only one thing: to preserve their privileges and to eliminate the nagging reminder that others have done and are doing better under freedom.

Every American president since World War II has known or quickly learned that the Soviet Union, for example, is not benign in its intentions.

The Soviet Union has no interest in maintaining the status quo. It does not accept our soft definition of "detente." To the Soviet Union, "detente" is an opportunity to expand its sphere of influence around the world.

The Soviet Union has steadily increased its capacity for such expansion. That capability has grown enormously since 1945 and, above all, since 1962 when the Cold War was first declared "over" by the hopeful and naive.

Today, the U.S.S.R. continues its drive to dominate the world in military capability: on land, on water, and in the air. Meanwhile, the Carter administration seems confused and torn, partly believing the realities and partly listening to those who believe that pre-emptive concession by the Soviets. But they don't bargain that way. They understand strength; they exploit weakness and take advantage of inexperience. And, possibly, it was inexperience that led the president to placate the most dovish members of his party by scuttling the B-1 bomber -- one of his bargaining chips -- even before the SALT II negotiations began.

One of the reasons given for cancellation of the B-1 was economy, and even here there was a lack of accuracy. First of all, the price given for the aircraft was what the price will be in 1986 if inflation continues -- which incidentally suggests a lack of resolve in the administration's anti-inflation fight. Second, we were told the B-52 or the F-111 could be modified to do the job the B-1 was supposed to do. Here the cost differential shrinks sizeably when we look at the facts. The modification itself is quite costly, and we can double that cost. It will take two planes to substitute for every B-1 because the B-1 carries twice the payload the others will. It will carry that load twice as fast in a plane only half the size of a B-52, and it is far less vulnerable to the Soviet defense system.

While confusion and conflicting advice seem to tug and pull at the White House, the Soviet Union continues to build up its capability for world domination. It has even gone so far as to put entire factories underground and to disperse much of its industrial capacity -- the most sophisticated civil defense program ever developed. The knowledge that our strategic missiles, if they ever had to be used, would inflict minimal damage on the Soviets, compared to the havoc theirs would produce on our continent, should, in itself, be sufficient to spur the administration to making certain that we be number one in the world in terms of national defense capabilities. So far, though, this does not seem to be a White House priority.

Today, we can see the brunt of the Soviet Union's capabilities at work in the Horn of Africa.

To most Americans, that part of the world seems remote, as Korea and Vietnam seemed remote, along with those other places where the Soviets have sought advantage.

In Ethiopia, formerly a close friend of the United States, the Soviets with their Cuban foreign legion have turned that country into a free-fire zone in order to subdue Ethiopia's two principal enemies, Somalia and the Eritrean rebels.

The Soviet goal is obvious: to secure a permanent foothold for itself on the Red Sea. If the Soviets are successful -- and it looks more and more as if they will be -- then the entire Horn of Africa will be under their influence, if not their control. From there, they can threaten the sea lanes carrying oil to western Europe and the United States, if and when they choose.

More immediately, control of the Horn of Africa would give Moscow the ability to destabilize those governments on the Arabian peninsula which have proven themselves strongly anti-Communist. Among them are some of the world's principal oil exporters.

Moscow can also turn its full attention south if it can ensure its position in the Horn of Africa. It takes no great stretch of the imagination to see that Rhodesia is a tempting target. Cuban leaders now boast that it is.

What are we doing about it? Apparently, our response to the Rhodesian settlement proposed by the moderate black leaders and Prime Minister Ian Smith is not to tell the Soviets -- behind the scenes -- to get lost or risk pressures elsewhere that they won't like. No, our response seems to be best summed up by our ambassador to the United Nations, who is unhappy with the moderate, democratic solution in Rhodesia because he's afraid (he says) it will bring on a massive Soviet arms buildup. What does he think we're having now? He seems to believe that the only Rhodesian plan we can afford to support is one to the liking of the two terrorist guerrilla leaders. But if they have their way, one or the other of them will become the sole power in Rhodesia, fronting of course for the Soviet Union. Unless we want to make the world safe for terrorist guerrillas, the only sensible course is for us to support the moderate solution in Rhodesia and quietly tell Moscow to keep its hands off -- unless, of course, we are too weak to do that. Is that what Mr. Young is trying to tell us? I hope not, for a Marxist

Rhodesia would lead to even more tempting targets for Moscow in Africa. Perhaps Djibouti, Sudan, Chad, the old Spanish Sahara (where guerrillas are already in operation).

And one other which will cost us dearly. Whatever we may think of South Africa's internal policies, control of its mineral riches and its strategic position are the Soviet Union's ultimate goal in Africa.

Unless the White House can bring itself to understand these realities, it is not too much to say that in a few years we may be faced with the prospect of a Soviet empire of proteges and dependencies stretching from Addis Ababa to Capetown. Those who now reject that possibility out of hand -- and they seem to have the ear of the man in the Oval Office -- have yet to explain Angola, Mozambique, the situation in the Horn of Africa or the terrorists in Rhodesia. One thing is certain: Soviet successes will not breed caution in the Kremlin. Rather, the reverse.

Those in the Carter administration who are not even inclined to protest the recent Soviet moves assure us that, sooner or later, the Soviets will make serious mistakes and our doing nothing will hasten that day.

But to say, as they do, that all is well because the Soviets are creating their own Vietnam is nonsense. These Carter advisers seem to forget that the Soviets won in Vietnam and they intend to win again -- this time in Africa. They learned the true lesson of the Vietnam war: certainty of purpose and ruthlessness of execution wins wars. Vietnam held no terror for the Soviets as it did for so many Americans. And, adventures in Africa hold no terror for them either.

To say, as some in the administration do, that African nationalism will stop the Soviets is the weakest reed of all. The reason is simple: African nationalism, as such, does not exist. No African government has yet condemned the Russians, nor do the halls of the Organization of African Unity ring with anti-Soviet slogans -- perhaps because those halls happen to be in Addis Ababa, the capital of Ethiopia.

The criticism by African states of the Soviets that the administration seems to be so desperately hoping for will not materialize. After all, there is in Africa, as around the world, a healthy respect for power and the determined use of power.

One veteran West European diplomat put the African situation in perspective recently. He was quoted as saying: "This situation is going to make the leaders of a lot of these small, weak nations stop and think. And what do they see on the American side? Apparent indecision, attempts to talk, a reluctance to give weapons to friends" -- and, he might have added, a "belief that there are nasty, immoral wars of imperialist aggression and nice clean wars of national liberation."

The administration's uncertainty of purpose isn't confined to the world's current hot spots. It is apparent even in our own hemisphere.

That White House tally sheet I mentioned listed its "accomplishments" in Latin America. It said, "The administration has developed a new global approach to Latin America...."

Well, what it has done from the beginning was to accept the notions fashionable in the most liberal circles that surrender of the

Panama Canal and rapprochement with Cuba were the keys to successful relations with Latin America.

Nothing could have been further from the truth. Of Panama, I have already had a good deal to say. But let me say again, we have earned no respect or lasting affection in Latin America with these treaties.

Unfortunately, our policy toward Latin America has not only entailed friendship for one dictator who is a sworn enemy and for another who routinely suppresses human rights and may be involved in the worst sort of corruption -- that policy has also entailed hostility toward our friends.

Let me cite just one example, Brazil. An ally in World War II, (contributing a division which saw hard action in Europe), a friend through most of the '60s and now a great hope for contributing to the future industrial strength of the West, Brazil now finds itself turned on by us -- with a vengeance. Whatever the motives, human rights or worries over nuclear proliferation, the ends did not justify the means. The result is that we have nearly lost a friend without achieving any of the administration's professed objectives.

It is time to try another approach, an approach based on reality and not the slogans and romantic notions of ideologues who just happen to have access to the Oval Office.

First, let us end this cycle of American indifference, followed by frenzied activity in Latin America (as it has been elsewhere). It leaves our southern neighbors bewildered and cynical. Instead, I propose a steadier course in which Latin America's growing importance is recognized not as an act of charity, but in our own self-interest. Latin America, with all its resources and vitality, should be encouraged to join not the Third World, much less the Communists' Second World, but the First World -- that community of stable, prosperous and free nations of Western Europe, North America and Japan.

Today, there is hope that much of Latin America might do so. First, many nations have learned the cost of Socialist experimentation: Argentina under the Perons, Chile under Allende, Peru under Velasco, Mexico under Echeverria. All suffered economic catastrophe. Their successors learned the bitter truth that defying the laws of economics benefits no one and, in fact, hurts most the poor whose cause those earlier leaders so demagogically espoused.

Today, as a result of those experiments which went so badly out of control, more and more of our neighbors are turning to the free market as a model of development. Their acceptance of economic rationality should be neither ignored nor penalized but actively encouraged.

At the same time, we must recognize that Latin America is once again leaving a period of strictly military rule and entering a more democratic phase. But in this case the United States is doing too much pushing, rather than too little.

Unhappily, the change from military to civilian rule is not an easy one. Nor can it be rushed. If it is, we will only succeed in creating weak and vulnerable democratic governments that will soon be swept out of power by just another generation of military strongmen even more convinced of the defects of democracy.

Above all, we want a free and prosperous Latin America. And, to obtain that, we cannot continue to reward our self-declared enemies and then turn around and punish our friends.

That leads me again to Panama. The treaties that have occupied so much of our attention in recent months represent both the good instincts and the bad impulses of American diplomacy.

The bad, for reasons I have repeated on many occasions: the feeling that we are guilty of some sin for which we must now atone and our inability to say "no," not out of truculence, but because it was the proper thing to say to secure our interests and to reaffirm our greater responsibility, which is leadership of all that remains of the free world.

Yes, the treaties represent the good instincts of American diplomacy, too -- a spirit of generosity and willingness to change with times. A good foreign policy must have both elements: the need to say "no" and the willingness to change, in just the right proportions. Unfortunately, accepting change because it seems fashionable to do so, with little real regard for the consequences, seems to dominate our foreign policy today.

Too many in positions of importance believe that through generosity and self-effacement we can avoid trouble, whether it's with Panama and the canal or the Soviet Union and SALT.

But, like it or not, trouble will not be avoided. The American people and their elected leaders will continue to be faced with hard choices and difficult moments, for resolve is continually being tested by those who envy us our prosperity and begrudge us our freedom.

America will remain great and act responsibly so long as it exercises power -- wisely, and not in the bullying sense -- but exercises it, nonetheless.

Leadership is a great burden. We grow weary of it at times. And the Carter administration, despite its own cheerful propaganda about accomplishments, reflects that weariness.

But if we are not to shoulder the burdens of leadership in the free world, then who will?

The alternatives are neither pleasant nor acceptable. Great nations which fail to meet their responsibilities are consigned to the dust bin of history. We grew from that small, weak republic which had as its assets spirit, optimism, faith in God and an unshakeable belief that free men and women could govern themselves wisely. We became the leader of the free world, an example for all those who cherish freedom.

If we are to continue to be that example -- if we are to preserve our own freedom -- we must understand those who would dominate us and deal with them with determination.

We must shoulder our burden with our eyes fixed on the future, but recognizing the realities of today, not counting on mere hope or wishes. We must be willing to carry out our responsibility as the custodian of individual freedom. Then we will achieve our destiny to be as a shining city on a hill for all mankind to see.

Official Announcement for President

November 13, 1979

Good evening. I am here tonight to announce my intention to seek the Republican nomination for President of the United States.

I'm sure that each of us has seen our country from a number of viewpoints, depending on where we've lived and what we've done. For me it has been as a boy growing up in several small towns in Illinois. As a young man in Iowa trying to get a start in the years of the Great Depression and later in California for most of my adult life.

I've seen America from the stadium press box as a sportscaster, as an actor, officer of my labor union, soldier, officeholder and as both a Democrat and Republican. I've lived in America where those who often had too little to eat outnumbered those who had enough. There have been four wars in my lifetime, and I've seen our country face financial ruin in the Depression. I have also seen the great strength of this nation as it pulled itself up from that ruin to become the dominant force in the world.

To me our country is a living, breathing presence, unimpressed by what others say is impossible, proud of its own success, generous -- yes and naïve -- sometimes wrong, never mean and always impatient to provide a better life for its people in a framework of a basic fairness and freedom.

Someone once said that the difference between an American and any other kind of person is that an American lives in anticipation of the future because he knows it will be a great place. Other people fear the future as just a repetition of past failures. There's a lot of truth in that. If there is one thing we are sure of it is that history need not be relived; that nothing is impossible, and that man is capable of improving his circumstances beyond what we are told is fact.

There are those in our land today, however, who would have us believe that the United States, like other great civilizations of the past, has reached the zenith of its power; that we are weak and fearful, reduced to bickering with each other and no longer possessed of the will to cope with our problems.

Much of this talk has come from leaders who claim that our problems are too difficult to handle. We are supposed to meekly accept their failures as the most which humanly can be done. They tell us we must learn to live with less, and teach our children that their lives will be less full and prosperous than ours have been; that the America of the coming years will be a place where -- because of our past excesses -- it will be impossible to dream and make those dreams come true.

I don't believe that. And I don't believe you do either. That is why I am seeking the presidency. I cannot and will not stand by and see this great country destroy itself. Our leaders attempt to blame their failures on circumstances beyond their control, on false estimates by unknown, unidentifiable experts who rewrite modern history in an attempt to convince us our high standard of living, the result of thrift and hard work, is somehow selfish extravagance which we must renounce as we join in sharing scarcity. I don't agree that our nation must resign itself to inevitable decline, yielding its proud position to other hands. I am totally unwilling to see this country fail in its obligation to itself and to the other free peoples of the world.

The crisis we face is not the result of any failure of the American spirit; it is failure of our leaders to establish rational goals and give our people something to order their lives by. If I am elected, I shall regard my election as proof that the people of the United States have decided to set a new agenda and have recognized that the human spirit thrives best when goals are set and progress can be measured in their achievement.

During the next year I shall discuss in detail a wide variety of problems which a new administration must address. Tonight I shall mention only a few.

No problem that we face today can compare with the need to restore the health of the American economy and the strength of the American dollar. Double-digit inflation has robbed you and your family of the ability to plan. It has destroyed the confidence to buy and it threatens the very structure of family life itself as more and more wives are forced to work in order to help meet the ever-increasing cost of living. At the same time, the lack of real growth in the economy has introduced the justifiable fear in the minds of working men and women who are already overextended that soon there will be fewer jobs and no money to pay for even the necessities of life. And tragically, as the cost of living keeps going up, the standard of living which has been our great pride keeps going down.

The people have not created this disaster in our economy; the federal government has. It has overspent, overestimated, and over-regulated. It has failed to deliver services within the revenues it should be allowed to raise from taxes. In the 34 years since the end of World War II, it has spent $448 billion more than it has collected in taxes -- $448 billion of printing-press money, which has made every dollar you earn worth less and less. At the same time, the federal government has cynically told us that high taxes on business will in some way "solve" the problem and allow the average taxpayer to pay less. Well, business is not a taxpayer; it is a tax collector. Business has to pass its tax burden on to the customer as part of the cost of doing business. You and I pay taxes imposed on business every time we go to the store. Only people pay taxes, and it is political demagoguery or economic illiteracy to try and tell us otherwise.

The key to restoring the health of the economy lies in cutting taxes. At the same time, we need to get the waste out of federal spending. This does not mean sacrificing essential services, nor do we need to destroy the system of benefits which flow to the poor, elderly, the sick and the handicapped. We have long since committed ourselves, as a people, to help those among us who cannot take care of themselves. But the federal government has proven to be the costliest and most inefficient provider of such help we could possibly have.

We must put an end to the arrogance of a federal establishment which accepts no blame for our condition, cannot be relied upon to give us a fair estimate of our situation and utterly refuses to live within its means. I will not accept the supposed "wisdom" which has it that the federal bureaucracy has become so powerful that it can no longer be changed or controlled by any administration. As President I would use every power at my command to make the federal establishment respond to the will and the collective wishes of the people.

We must force the entire federal bureaucracy to live in the real world of reduced spending, streamlined function and accountability to the people it serves. We must review the function of the federal government to determine which of those are the proper province of levels of government closer to the people.

The 10th article of the Bill of Rights is explicit in pointing out that the federal government should do only those things specifically called for in the Constitution. All others shall remain with the states or the people. We haven't been observing that 10th article of late. The federal government has taken on functions it was never intended to perform and which it does not perform well. There should be a planned, orderly transfer of such functions to states and communities and a transfer with them of the sources of taxation to pay for them.

The savings in administrative overhead would be considerable and certainly there would be increased efficiency and less bureaucracy.

By reducing federal tax rates where they discourage individual initiative -- especially personal income tax rates -- we can restore incentives, invite greater economic growth and at the same time help give us better government instead of bigger government. Proposals such as the Kemp-Roth bill would bring about this kind of realistic reductions in tax rates.

In short, a punitive tax system must be replaced by one that restores incentive for the worker and for industry -- a system that rewards initiative and effort and encourages thrift.

All these things are possible; none of them will be easy. But the choice is clear. We can go on letting the country slip over the brink to financial ruin with the disaster that it means for the individual or we can find the will to work together to restore confidence in ourselves and to regain the confidence of the world. I have lived through one Depression. I carry with me the memory of a Christmas Eve when my brother and I and our parents exchanged our modest gifts -- there was no lighted tree as there has been on Christmases past. I remember watching my father open what he thought was a greeting from his employer. We all watched and yes, we were hoping it was a bonus check. It was notice that he no longer had a job. And in those days the government ran the radio announcements telling workers not to leave home looking for jobs -- there were no jobs. I'll carry with me always the memory of my father sitting there holding that envelope, unable to look at us. I cannot and will not stand by while inflation and joblessness destroy the dignity of our people.

Another serious problem which must be discussed tonight is our energy situation. Our country was built on cheap energy. Today, energy is not cheap and we face the prospect that some forms of energy may soon not be available at all.

Last summer you probably spent hours sitting in gasoline lines. This winter, some will be without heat and everyone will be paying much more simply to keep home and family warm. If you ever had any doubt of the government's inability to provide for the needs of the people, just look at the utter fiasco we now call "the energy crisis." Not one straight answer nor any realistic hope of relief has come from the present administration in almost three years of federal treatment of the problem. As gas lines grew, the administration again panicked and now has proposed to put the country on a wartime footing; but for this "war" there is no victory in sight. And, as always, when the federal bureaucracy fails, all it can suggest is more of the same. This time it's another bureau to untangle the mess by the ones we already have.

But, this just won't work. Solving the energy crisis will not be easy, but it can be done. First we must decide that "less" is not enough. Next, we must remove government obstacles to energy production. And we must make use of those technological advantages we still possess.

It is no program simply to say, "Use less energy." Of course waste must be eliminated and efficiently promoted, but for the government simply to tell people to conserve is not an energy policy. At best it means we will run out of energy a little more slowly. But a day will come when the lights will dim and the wheels of industry will turn more slowly and finally stop. As President I will not endorse any course which has this as its principal objective.

We need more energy and that means diversifying our sources of supply away from the OPEC countries. Yes, it means more efficient automobiles. But it also means more exploration and development of oil and natural gas here in our own country. The only way to free ourselves from the monopoly pricing power of OPEC is to be less dependent on outside sources of fuel.

The answer, obvious to anyone except those in the administration it seems, is more domestic production of oil and gas. We must also have wider use of nuclear power within strict safety rules, of course. There must be more spending by the energy industries on research and development of substitutes for fossil fuels.

In years to come solar energy may provide much of the answer but for the next two or three decades we must do such things as master the chemistry of coal. Putting the market system to work for these objectives is an essential first step for their achievement. Additional multi-billion-dollar federal bureaus and programs are not the answer.

In recent weeks there has been much talk about "excess" oil company profits. I don't believe we've been given all the information we need to make a judgment about this. We should have that information. Government exists to protect us from each other. It is not government's function to allocate fuel or impose unnecessary restrictions on the marketplace. It is government's function to determine whether we are being unfairly exploited and if so to take immediate and appropriate action. As President I would do exactly that.

On the foreign front, the decade of the 1980s will place severe pressures upon the United States and its allies. We can expect to be tested in ways calculated to try our patience, to confound our resolve and to erode our belief in ourselves. During a time when the Soviet Union may enjoy nuclear superiority over this country, we must never waiver in our commitment to our allies nor accept any negotiation which is not clearly in the national interest. We must judge carefully. Though we should leave no initiative untried in our pursuit of peace, we must be clear voiced in our resolve to resist any unpeaceful act wherever it may occur. Negotiation with the Soviet Union must never become appeasement.

For the most of the last 40 years, we have been preoccupied with the global struggle -- the competition -- with the Soviet Union and with our responsibilities to our allies. But too often in recent times we have just drifted along with events, responding as if we thought of ourselves as a nation in decline. To our allies we seem to appear to be a nation unable to make decisions in its own interests, let alone in the common interest. Since the Second World War we have spent large amounts of money and much of our time protecting and defending freedom all over the world. We must continue this, for if we do not accept the responsibilities of leadership, who will? And if no one will, how will we survive?

The 1970s have taught us the foolhardiness of not having a long-range diplomatic strategy of our own. The world has become a place where, in order to survive, our country needs more than just allies -- it needs real friends. Yet, in recent times we often seem not to have recognized who our friends are. This must change. It is now time to take stock of our own house and to re-supply its strength.

Part of that process involves taking stock of our relationship with Puerto Rico. I favor statehood for Puerto Rico and if the people of Puerto Rico vote for statehood in their coming referendum I would, as President, initiate the enabling legislation to make this a reality.

We live on a continent whose three countries possess the assets to make it the strongest, most prosperous and self-sufficient area on Earth. Within the borders of this North American continent are the food, resources, technology and undeveloped territory which, properly managed, could dramatically improve the quality of life of all its inhabitants.

It is no accident that this unmatched potential for progress and prosperity exists in three countries with such long-standing heritages of free government. A developing closeness among

Canada, Mexico and the United States -- a North American accord -- would permit achievement of that potential in each country beyond that which I believe any of them -- strong as they are -- could accomplish in the absence of such cooperation. In fact, the key to our own future security may lie in both Mexico and Canada becoming much stronger countries than they are today.

No one can say at this point precisely what form future cooperation among our three countries will take. But if I am elected President, I would be willing to invite each of our neighbors to send a special representative to our government to sit in on high level planning sessions with us, as partners, mutually concerned about the future of our continent. First, I would immediately seek the views and ideas of Canadian and Mexican leaders on this issue, and work tirelessly with them to develop closer ties among our peoples. It is time we stopped thinking of our nearest neighbors as foreigners.

By developing methods of working closely together, we will lay the foundations for future cooperation on a broader and more significant scale. We will put to rest any doubts of those cynical enough to believe that the United States would seek to dominate any relationship among our three countries, or foolish enough to think that the governments and peoples of Canada and Mexico would ever permit such domination to occur. I, for one, am confident that we can show the world by example that the nations of North America are ready, within the context of an unswerving commitment to freedom, to see new forms of accommodation to meet a changing world. A developing closeness between the United States, Canada and Mexico would serve notice on friends and foe alike that we were prepared for a long haul, looking outward again and confident of our future; that together we are going to create jobs, to generate new fortunes of wealth for many and provide a legacy for the children of each of our countries. Two hundred years ago, we taught the world that a new form of government, created out of the genius of man to cope with his circumstances, could succeed in bringing a measure of quality to human life previously thought impossible.

Now let us work toward the goal of using the assets of this continent, its resources, technology, and foodstuffs in the most efficient ways possible for the common good of all its people. It may take the next 100 years, but we can dare to dream that at some future date a map of the world might show the North American continent as one in which the people's commerce of its three strong countries flow more freely across their present borders than they do today.

In recent months leaders in our government have told us that, we, the people, have lost confidence in ourselves; that we must regain our spirit and our will to achieve our national goals. Well, it is true there is a lack of confidence, an unease with things the way they are. But the confidence we have lost is confidence in our government's policies. Our unease can almost be called bewilderment at how our defense strength has deteriorated. The great productivity of our industry is now surpassed by virtually all the major nations who compete with us for world markets. And, our currency is no longer the stable measure of value it once was.

But there remains the greatness of our people, our capacity for dreaming up fantastic deeds and bringing them off to the surprise of an unbelieving world. When Washington's men were freezing at

Valley Forge, Tom Paine told his fellow Americans: "We have it in our power to begin the world over again." We still have that power.

We -- today's living Americans -- have in our lifetime fought harder, paid a higher price for freedom and done more to advance the dignity of man than any people who have ever lived on this Earth. The citizens of this great nation want leadership, yes, but not a "man on a white horse" demanding obedience to his commands. They want someone who believes they can "begin the world over again." A leader who will unleash their great strength and remove the roadblocks government has put in their way. I want to do that more than anything I've ever wanted. And it's something that I believe with God's help I can do.

I believe this nation hungers for a spiritual revival; hungers to once again see honor placed above political expediency; to see government once again the protector of our liberties, not the distributor of gifts and privilege. Government should uphold and not undermine those institutions which are custodians of the very values upon which civilization is founded -- religion, education and, above all, family. Government cannot be clergyman, teacher and patriot. It is our servant, beholden to us.

We who are privileged to be Americans have had a rendezvous with destiny since the moment in 1630 when John Winthrop, standing on the deck of the tiny Arbella off the coast of Massachusetts, told the little band of Pilgrims, "We shall be a city upon a hill. The eyes of all people are upon us so that if we shall deal falsely with our God in this work we have undertaken and so cause Him to withdraw His present help from us, we shall be made a story and a byword throughout the world."

A troubled and afflicted mankind looks to us, pleading for us to keep our rendezvous with destiny; that we will uphold the principles of self-reliance, self-discipline, morality, and -- above all -- responsible liberty for every individual that we will become that shining city on a hill.

I believe that you and I together can keep this rendezvous with destiny.

Thank you and good night.

Christmas Address of President Reagan

December 23, 1981

Good evening.

At Christmas time, every home takes on a special beauty, a special warmth, and that's certainly true of the White House, where so many famous Americans have spent their Christmases over the years. This fine old home, the people's house, has seen so much, been so much a part of all our lives and history. It's been humbling and inspiring for Nancy and me to be spending our first Christmas in this place.

We've lived here as your tenants for almost a year now, and what a year it's been. As a people we've been through quite a lot -- moments of joy, of tragedy, and of real achievement -- moments that I believe have brought us all closer together. G. K. Chesterton once said that the world would never starve for wonders, but only for the want of wonder.

At this special time of year, we all renew our sense of wonder in recalling the story of the first Christmas in Bethlehem, nearly 2,000 year ago.

Some celebrate Christmas as the birthday of a great and good philosopher and teacher. Others of us believe in the divinity of the child born in Bethlehem, that he was and is the promised Prince of Peace. Yes, we've questioned why he who could perform miracles chose to come among us as a helpless babe, but maybe that was his first miracle, his first great lesson that we should learn to care for one another.

Tonight, in millions of American homes, the glow of the Christmas tree is a reflection of the love Jesus taught us. Like the shepherds and wise men of that first Christmas, we Americans have always tried to follow a higher light, a star, if you will. At lonely campfire vigils along the frontier, in the darkest days of the Great Depression, through war and peace, the twin beacons of faith and freedom have brightened the American sky. At times our footsteps may have faltered, but trusting in God's help, we've never lost our way.

Just across the way from the White House stand the two great emblems of the holiday season: a Menorah, symbolizing the Jewish festival of Hanukkah, and the National Christmas Tree, a beautiful towering blue spruce from Pennsylvania. Like the National Christmas Tree, our country is a living, growing thing planted in rich American soil. Only our devoted care can bring it to full flower. So, let this holiday season be for us a time of rededication.

Even as we rejoice, however, let us remember that for some Americans, this will not be as happy a Christmas as it should be. I know a little of what they feel. I remember one Christmas Eve during the Great Depression, my father opening what he thought was a Christmas greeting. It was a notice that he no longer had a job.

Over the past year, we've begun the long, hard work of economic recovery. Our goal is an America in which every citizen who needs and wants a job can get a job. Our program for recovery has only been in place for 12 weeks now, but it is beginning to work. With your help and prayers, it will succeed. We're winning the battle against inflation, runaway government spending and taxation, and that victory will mean more economic growth, more jobs, and more opportunity for all Americans.

A few months before he took up residence in this house, one of my predecessors, John Kennedy, tried to sum up the temper of the times with a quote from an author closely tied to Christmas, Charles Dickens. We were living, he said, in the best of times and the worst of times. Well, in some ways that's even more true today. The world is full of peril, as well as promise. Too many of its people, even now, live in the shadow of want and tyranny.

As I speak to you tonight, the fate of a proud and ancient nation hangs in the balance. For a thousand years, Christmas has been celebrated in Poland, a land of deep religious faith, but this Christmas brings little joy to the courageous Polish people. They have been betrayed by their own government.

The men who rule them and their totalitarian allies fear the very freedom that the Polish people cherish. They have answered the stirrings of liberty with brute force, killings, mass arrests, and the setting up of concentration camps. Lech Walesa and other Solidarity leaders are imprisoned, their fate unknown. Factories, mines, universities, and homes have been assaulted.

The Polish Government has trampled underfoot solemn commitments to the UN Charter and the Helsinki accords. It has even broken the Gdansk agreement of August 1980, by which the Polish Government recognized the basic right of its people to form free trade unions and to strike.

The tragic events now occurring in Poland, almost 2 years to the day after the Soviet invasion of Afghanistan, have been precipitated by public and secret pressure from the Soviet Union. It is no coincidence that Soviet Marshal Kulikov, chief of the Warsaw Pact forces, and other senior Red Army officers were in Poland while these outrages were being initiated. And it is no coincidence that the martial law proclamations imposed in December by the Polish Government were being printed in the Soviet Union in September.

The target of this depression [repression] is the Solidarity Movement, but in attacking Solidarity its enemies attack an entire people. Ten million of Poland's 36 million citizens are members of Solidarity. Taken together with their families, they account for the overwhelming majority of the Polish nation. By persecuting Solidarity the Polish Government wages war against its own people.

I urge the Polish Government and its allies to consider the consequences of their actions. How can they possibly justify using naked force to crush a people who ask for nothing more than the right to lead their own lives in freedom and dignity? Brute force may intimidate, but it cannot form the basis of an enduring society, and the ailing Polish economy cannot be rebuilt with terror tactics.

Poland needs cooperation between its government and its people, not military oppression. If the Polish Government will honor the commitments it has made to human rights in documents like the Gdansk agreement, we in America will gladly do our share to help the shattered Polish economy, just as we helped the countries of Europe after both World Wars.

It's ironic that we offered, and Poland expressed interest in accepting, our help after World War II. The Soviet Union intervened then and refused to allow such help to Poland. But if the forces of tyranny in Poland, and those who incite them from without, do not relent, they should prepare themselves for serious consequences. Already, throughout the Free World, citizens have publicly demonstrated their support for the Polish people. Our government, and those of our allies, have expressed moral revulsion at the police state tactics of Poland's oppressors. The Church has also spoken out, in spite of threats and intimidation. But our reaction cannot stop there.

I want emphatically to state tonight that if the outrages in Poland do not cease, we cannot and will not conduct ``business as usual'' with the perpetrators and those who aid and abet them. Make no mistake, their crime will cost them dearly in their future dealings with America and free peoples everywhere. I do not make this statement lightly or without serious reflection.

We have been measured and deliberate in our reaction to the tragic events in Poland. We have not acted in haste, and the steps I will outline tonight and others we may take in the days ahead are firm, just, and reasonable.

In order to aid the suffering Polish people during this critical period, we will continue the shipment of food through private humanitarian channels, but only so long as we know that the Polish people themselves receive the food. The neighboring country of Austria has opened her doors to refugees from Poland. I have therefore directed that American assistance, including supplies of basic foodstuffs, be offered to aid the Austrians in providing for these refugees.

But to underscore our fundamental opposition to the repressive actions taken by the Polish Government against its own people, the administration has suspended all government-sponsored shipments of agricultural and dairy products to the Polish Government. This suspension will remain in force until absolute assurances are received that distribution of these products is monitored and guaranteed by independent agencies. We must be sure that every bit of food provided by America goes to the Polish people, not to their oppressors.

The United States is taking immediate action to suspend major elements of our economic relationships with the Polish Government. We have halted the renewal of the Export-Import Bank's line of export credit insurance to the Polish Government. We will suspend Polish civil aviation privileges in the United States. We are suspending the right of Poland's fishing fleet to operate in American waters. And we're proposing to our allies the further restriction of high technology exports to Poland.

These actions are not directed against the Polish people. They are a warning to the Government of Poland that free men cannot and will not stand idly by in the face of brutal repression. To underscore this point, I've written a letter to General Jaruzelski, head of the Polish Government. In it, I outlined the steps we're taking and warned of the serious consequences if the Polish Government continues to use violence against its populace. I've urged him to free those in arbitrary detention, to lift martial law, and to restore the internationally recognized rights of the Polish people to free speech and association.

The Soviet Union, through its threats and pressures, deserves a major share of blame for the developments in Poland. So, I have also sent a letter to President Brezhnev urging him to permit the restoration of basic human rights in Poland provided for in the Helsinki Final Act. In it, I informed him that if this repression continues, the United States will have no choice but to take further concrete political and economic measures affecting our relationship.

When 19th century Polish patriots rose against foreign oppressors, their rallying cry was, ``For our freedom and yours.'' Well, that motto still rings true in our time. There is a spirit of solidarity abroad in the world tonight that no physical force can crush. It crosses national boundaries and enters into the hearts of men and women everywhere. In factories, farms, and schools, in cities and towns around the globe, we the people of the Free World stand as one with our Polish brothers and sisters. Their cause is ours, and our prayers and hopes go out to them this Christmas.

Yesterday, I met in this very room with Romuald Spasowski, the distinguished former Polish Ambassador who has sought asylum in our country in protest of the suppression of his native land. He told me that one of the ways the Polish people have demonstrated their solidarity in the face of martial law is by placing lighted candles in their windows to show that the light of liberty still glows in their hearts.

Ambassador Spasowski requested that on Christmas Eve a lighted candle will burn in the White House window as a small but certain beacon of our solidarity with the Polish people. I urge all of you to do the same tomorrow night, on Christmas Eve, as a personal statement of your commitment to the steps we're taking to support the brave people of Poland in their time of troubles.

Once, earlier in this century, an evil influence threatened that the lights were going out all over the world. Let the light of millions of candles in American homes give notice that the light of freedom is not going to be extinguished. We are blessed with a freedom and abundance denied to so many. Let those candles remind us that these blessings bring with them a solid obligation, an obligation to the God who guides us, an obligation to the heritage of liberty and dignity handed down to us by our forefathers and an obligation to the children of the world, whose future will be shaped by the way we live our lives today.

Christmas means so much because of one special child. But Christmas also reminds us that all children are special, that they are gifts from God, gifts beyond price that mean more than any presents money can buy. In their love and laughter, in our hopes for their future lies the true meaning of Christmas.

So, in a spirit of gratitude for what we've been able to achieve together over the past year and looking forward to all that we hope to achieve together in the years ahead, Nancy and I want to wish you all the best of holiday seasons. As Charles Dickens, whom I quoted a few moments ago, said so well in ``A Christmas Carol,'' ``God bless us, every one.''

Good night.

Ronald Wilson Reagan taking the Oath of Office
as Our 40th President of the United States, January 1981

President Ronald Reagan delivers his First Inaugural Address

President & Mrs. Reagan
Leading the Crusade to Make America Great Again!

President Ronald Reagan Passes in Review of the troops he loved ...
and we loved him, too!

President Reagan speaking to soldiers in South Korea

President & Mrs. Reagan preparing for Christmas at the White House

President & Mrs. Reagan lifting the spirits
and doing the hard work necessary to Make America Great Again!

President Reagan honoring the fallen

President Reagan addresses the Nation before the Statue of Liberty, with First Lady Nancy Reagan looking on

President Reagan sharing a light-hearted moment with William F. Buckley, Jr.

President Reagan takes Oath of Office at Second Inaugural, January 1985

The Commander in Chief respecting and thanking the troops

President Reagan seconds before delivering his Farewell Address

President Reagan's Funeral Procession, with First Lady Nancy Reagan

... for Everything!

First State of the Union Address

January 26, 1982

Thank you. Mr. Speaker, thank you. Thank you very much. Mr. Speaker, Mr. President, Distinguished Members of the Congress, honored guests and fellow citizens:

Today marks my first State of the Union address to you, a constitutional duty as old as our republic itself.

President Washington began this tradition in 1790 after reminding the nation that the destiny of self-government and the "preservation of the sacred fire of liberty" is "finally staked on the experiment entrusted to the hands of the American people." For our friends in the press, who place a high premium on accuracy, let me say: I did not actually hear George Washington say that, but it is a matter of historic record.

But from this podium, Winston Churchill asked the free world to stand together against the onslaught of aggression. Franklin Delano Roosevelt spoke of a day of infamy and summoned a nation to arms. And Douglas MacArthur made an unforgettable farewell to a country he had loved and served so well. Dwight Eisenhower reminded us that peace was purchased only at the price of strength and John F. Kennedy spoke of the burden and glory that is freedom.

When I visited this chamber last year as a newcomer to Washington, critical of past policies which I believe had failed, I proposed a new spirit of partnership between this Congress and this Administration and between Washington and our state and local governments.

In forging this new partnership for America we could achieve the oldest hopes of our republic, prosperity for our nation, peace for the world, and the blessings of individual liberty for our children and, someday, for all of humanity.

It's my duty to report to you tonight on the progress that we have made in our relations with other nations, on the foundation we've carefully laid for our economic recovery and, finally, on a bold and spirited initiative that I believe can change the face of American government and make it again the servant of the people.

Seldom have the stakes been higher for America. What we do and say here will make all the difference to auto workers in Detroit, lumberjacks in the Northwest, steelworkers in Steubenville who are in the unemployment lines, to black teen-agers in Newark and Chicago; to hard-pressed farmers and small businessmen and to millions of everyday Americans who harbor the simple wish of a safe and financially secure future for their children.

To understand the State of the Union, we must look not only at where we are and where we're going but where we've been. The situation at this time last year was truly ominous.

The last decade has seen a series of recessions. There was a recession in 1970, in 1974, and again in the spring of 1980. Each time, unemployment increased and inflation soon turned up again. We coined the word "stagflation" to describe this.

Government's response to these recessions was to pump up the money supply and increase spending.

In the last six months of 1980, as an example, the money supply increased at the fastest rate in postwar history, 13 percent. Inflation remained in double digits, and government spending increased at an annual rate of 17 percent. Interest rates reached a staggering 21 1/2 percent. There were eight million unemployed.

Late in 1981, we sank into the present recession largely because continued high interest rates hurt the auto industry and construction. And there was a drop in productivity and the already high unemployment increased.

This time, however, things are different. We have an economic program in place completely different from the artificial quick-fixes of the past. It calls for a reduction of the rate of increase in government spending, and already that rate has been cut nearly in half. But reduced spending alone isn't enough. We've just implemented the first and smallest phase of a three-year tax-rate reduction designed to stimulate the economy and create jobs.

Already interest rates are down to 15 3/4 percent, but they must still go lower. Inflation is down from 12.4 percent to 8.9, and for the month of December it was running at an annualized rate of 5.2 percent.

If we had not acted as we did, things would be far worse for all Americans than they are today. Inflation, taxes and interest rates would all be higher.

A year ago, Americans' faith in their governmental process was steadily declining. Six out of ten Americans were saying they were pessimistic about their future.

A new kind of defeatism was heard. Some said our domestic problems were uncontrollable, that we had to learn to live with the seemingly endless cycle of high inflation and high unemployment.

There were also pessimistic predictions about the relationship between our Administration and this Congress. It was said we could never work together. Well, those predictions were wrong. The record is clear, and I believe that history will remember this as an era of American renewal, remember this Administration as an Administration of change and remember this Congress as a Congress of destiny.

Together, we not only cut the increase in government spending nearly in half, we brought about the largest tax reductions and the most sweeping changes in our tax structure since the beginning of this century. And because we indexed future taxes to the rate of inflation, we took away government's built-in profit on inflation and its hidden incentive to grow larger at the expense of American workers.

Together, after 50 years of taking power away from the hands of the people in their states and local communities we have started returning power and resources to them.

Together, we have cut the growth of new Federal regulations nearly in half. In 1981, there were 23,000 fewer pages in the Federal Register, which lists new regulations, than there were in 1980. By deregulating oil, we've come closer to achieving energy independence and help bring down the costs of gasoline and heating fuel.

Together, we have created an effective Federal strike force to combat waste and fraud in government. In just six months it has saved the taxpayers more than $2 billion, and it's only getting started.

Together, we've begun to mobilize the private sector not to duplicate wasteful and discredited government programs but to bring thousands of Americans into a volunteer effort to help solve many of America's social problems.

Together, we've begun to restore that margin of military safety that insures peace. Our country's uniform is being worn once again with pride.

Together we have made a new beginning, but we have only begun.

No one pretends that the way ahead will be easy. In my inaugural address last year, I warned that the "ills we suffer have come upon us over several decades. They will not go away in days, weeks or months, but they will go away . . . because we as Americans have the capacity now, as we've had it in the past, to do whatever needs to be done to preserve this last and greatest bastion of freedom."

The economy will face difficult moments in the months ahead. But, the program for economic recovery that is in place will pull the economy out of its slump and put us on the road to prosperity and stable growth by the latter half of this year.

That is why I can report to you tonight that in the near future the State of the Union and the economy will be better much better if we summon the strength to continue on the course that we've charted.

And so the question: If the fundamentals are in place, what now?

Two things. First, we must understand what's happening at the moment to the economy. Our current problems are not the product of the recovery program that's only just now getting under way, as some would have you believe; they are the inheritance of decades of tax and tax, and spend and spend.

Second, because our economic problems are deeply rooted and will not respond to quick political fixes, we must stick to our carefully integrated plan for recovery. And that plan is based on four common-sense fundamentals: continued reduction of the growth in Federal spending, preserving the individual and business tax deductions that will stimulate saving and investment, removing unnecessary Federal regulations to spark productivity and maintaining a healthy dollar and a stable monetary policy, the latter a responsibility of the Federal Reserve System.

The only alternative being offered to this economic program is a return to the policies that gave us a trillion-dollar debt, runaway inflation, runaway interest rates and unemployment.

The doubters would have us turn back the clock with tax increases that would offset the personal tax-rate reductions already passed by this Congress.

Raise present taxes to cut future deficits, they tell us. Well, I don't believe we should buy that argument. There are too many imponderables for anyone to predict deficits or surpluses several years ahead with any degree of accuracy. The budget in place when I took office had been projected as balanced. It turned out to have one of the biggest deficits in history. Another example of the imponderables that can make deficit projections highly questionable: A change of only one percentage point in unemployment can alter a deficit up or down by some $25 billion.

As it now stands, our forecasts, which we're required by law to make, will show major deficits, starting at less than $100 billion and declining, but still too high.

More important, we are making progress with the three keys to reducing deficits: economic growth, lower interest rates and spending control. The policies we have in place will reduce the deficit steadily, surely and, in time, completely.

Higher taxes would not mean lower deficits. If they did, how would we explain tax revenues more than doubled just since 1976, yet in that same six-year period we ran the largest series of deficits in our history? In 1980 tax revenues increased by $54 billion, and in 1980 we had one of our all-time biggest deficits.

Raising taxes won't balance the budget. It will encourage more government spending and less private investment. Raising taxes will slow economic growth, reduce production and destroy future jobs, making it more difficult for those without jobs to find them and more likely that those who now have jobs could lose them.

So I will not ask you to try to balance the budget on the backs of the American taxpayers. I will seek no tax increases this year and I have no intention of retreating from our basic program of tax relief. I promised the American people to bring their tax rates down and keep them down to provide them incentives to rebuild our economy, to save, to invest in America's future. I will stand by my word. Tonight I'm urging the American people: Seize these new opportunities to produce, to save, to invest, and together we'll make this economy a mighty engine of freedom, hope and prosperity again.

Now the budget deficit this year will exceed our earlier expectations. The recession did that. It lowered revenues and increased costs. To some extent, we're also victims of our own success. We've brought inflation down faster than we thought we could and in doing this we've deprived government of those hidden revenues that occur when inflation pushes people into higher income tax brackets. And the continued high interest rates last year cost the government about $5 billion more than anticipated.

We must cut out more nonessential government spending and root out more waste, and we will continue our efforts to reduce the number of employees in the Federal work force by 75,000.

Starting in fiscal 1984, the Federal Government will assume full responsibility for the cost of the rapidly growing Medicaid program to go along with its existing responsibility for Medicare. As part of a financially equal swap, the states will simultaneously take full responsibility for Aid to Families With Dependent Children and food stamps. This will make welfare less costly and more responsive to genuine need because it will be designed and administered closer to the grass roots and the people it serves.

In 1984, the Federal Government will apply the full proceeds from certain excise taxes to a grassroots trust fund that will belong, in fair shares, to the 50 states. The total amount flowing into this fund will be $28 billion a year.

Over the next four years, the states can use this money in either of two ways. If they want to continue receiving Federal grants in such areas as transportation, education and social services, they can use their trust fund money to pay for the grants or, to the extent they choose to forgo the Federal grant programs, they can use their trust fund money on their own, for those or other purposes. There will be a mandatory pass-through of part of these funds to local governments.

By 1988, the states will be in complete control of over 40 Federal grant programs. The trust fund will start to phase out, eventually to disappear, and the excise taxes will be turned over to the states. They can then preserve, lower or raise taxes on their own and fund and manage these programs as they see fit.

In a single stroke, we will be accomplishing a real realignment that will end cumbersome administration and spiraling costs at the Federal level while we insure these programs will be more responsive to both the people they're meant to help and the people who pay for them.

Hand in hand with this program to strengthen the discretion and flexibility of state and local governments, we're proposing legislation for an experimental effort to improve and develop our depressed urban areas in the 1980's and 1990's. This legislation will permit states and localities to apply to the Federal Government for designation as urban enterprise zones. A broad range of special economic incentives in the zones will help attract new business, new jobs, new opportunity to America's inner cities and rural towns. Some will say our mission is to save free enterprise. Well, I say we must free enterprise so that, together, we can save America.

Some will also say our states and local communities are not up to the challenge of a new and creative partnership. Well, that might have been true 20 years ago before reforms like reapportionment and the Voting Rights Act, the 10-year extension of which I strongly support. It's no longer true today. This Administration has faith in state and local governments and the constitutional balance envisioned by the Founding Fathers. We also believe in the integrity, decency and sound good sense of grassroots Americans.

Our faith in the American people is reflected in another major endeavor. Our private sector initiatives task force is seeking out successful community models of school, church, business, union, foundation and civic programs that help community needs. Such groups are almost invariably far more efficient than government in running social programs.

We're not asking them to replace discarded and often discredited government programs dollar for dollar, service for service. We just want to help them perform the good works they choose, and help others to profit by their example. Three hundred eighty-five thousand corporations and private organizations are already working on social programs ranging from drug rehabilitation to job training, and thousands more Americans have written us asking how they can help. The volunteer spirit is still alive and well in America.

Our nation's long journey towards civil rights for all our citizens, once a source of discord, now a source of pride, must continue with no back sliding or slowing down. We must and shall see that those basic laws that guarantee equal rights are preserved and, when necessary, strengthened. Our concern for equal rights for women is firm and unshakable.

We launched a new Task Force on Legal Equity for Women, and a 50-states project that will examine state laws for discriminatory language. And for the first time in our history a woman sits on the highest court in the land.

So, too, the problem of crime, one as real and deadly serious as any in America today; it demands that we seek transformation of our legal system, which overly protects the rights of criminals while it leaves society and the innocent victims of crime without justice.

We look forward to the enactment of a responsible Clean Air Act to increase jobs while continuing to improve the quality of our air. We are encouraged by the bipartisan initiative of the House and are hopeful of further progress as the Senate continues its deliberations.

So far I have concentrated largely now on domestic matters. To view the State of the Union in perspective, we must not ignore the rest of the world. There isn't time tonight for a lengthy treatment of social or of foreign policy, I should say a subject I intend to address in detail in the near future. A few words, however, are in order on the progress we've made over the past year re-establishing respect for our nation around the globe and some of the challenges and goals that we will approach in the year ahead.

At Ottawa and Cancun, I met with leaders of the major industrial powers and developing nations. Now some of those I met with were a little surprised I didn't apologize for America's wealth. Instead I spoke of the strength of the free marketplace system and how that system could help them realize their aspirations for economic development and political freedom. I believe lasting friendships were made and the foundation was laid for future cooperation.

In the vital region of the Caribbean Basin, we're developing a program of aid, trade and investment incentives to promote self-sustaining growth and a better, more secure life for our neighbors to the south. Toward those who would export terrorism and subversion in the Caribbean and elsewhere, especially Cuba and Libya, we will act with firmness.

Our foreign policy is a policy of strength, fairness and balance. By restoring America's military credibility, by pursuing peace at the negotiating table wherever both sides are willing to sit down in good faith, and by regaining the respect of America's allies and adversaries alike, we have strengthened our country's position as a force for peace and progress in the world.

When action is called for, we're taking it. Our sanctions against the military dictatorship that has attempted to crush human rights in Poland and against the Soviet regime behind the military dictatorship clearly demonstrated to the world that America will not conduct "business as usual" with the forces of oppression.

If the events in Poland continue to deteriorate, further measures will follow.

The budget plan I submit to you on Feb. 8 will realize major savings by dismantling the Departments of Energy and Education, and by eliminating ineffective subsidies for business. We will continue to redirect our resources to our two highest budget priorities: a strong national defense to keep America free and at peace and a reliable safety net of social programs for those who have contributed and those who are in need.

Contrary to some of the wild charges you may have heard, this Administration has not and will not turn its back on America's elderly or America's poor. Under the new budget, funding for social insurance programs will be more than double the amount spent only six years ago.

But it would be foolish to pretend that these or any programs cannot be made more efficient and economical.

The entitlement programs that make up our safety net for the truly needy have worthy goals and many deserving recipients. We will protect them. But there's only one way to see to it that these programs really help those whom they were designed to help, and that is to bring their spiraling costs under control.

Today we face the absurd situation of a Federal budget with three-quarters of its expenditures routinely referred to as "uncontrollable," and a large part of this goes to entitlement programs.

Committee after committee of this Congress has heard witness after witness describe many of these programs as poorly administered and rife with waste and fraud. Virtually every American who shops in a local supermarket is aware of the daily abuses that take place in the food stamp program, which has grown by 16,000 percent in the last 15 years. Another example is Medicare and Medicaid, programs with worthy goals but whose costs have increased from 11.2 billion to almost 60 billion, more than five times as much, in just 10 years.

Waste and fraud are serious problems. Back in 1980, Federal investigators testified before one of your committees that "corruption has permeated virtually every area of the Medicare and Medicaid health care industry." One official said many of the people who are cheating the system were "very confident that nothing was going to happen to them."

Well, something is going to happen. Not only the taxpayers are defrauded, the people with real dependency on these programs are deprived of what they need because available resources are going not to the needy but to the greedy.

The time has come to control the uncontrollable.

In August we made a start. I signed a bill to reduce the growth of these programs by $44 billion over the next three years, while at the same time preserving essential services for the truly needy. Shortly you will receive from me a message on further reforms we intend to install, some new, but others long recommended by your own Congressional committees. I ask you to help make these savings for the American taxpayer.

The savings we propose in entitlement programs will total some $63 billion over four years and will, without affecting Social Security, go a long way toward bringing Federal spending under control.

But don't be fooled by those who proclaim that spending cuts will deprive the elderly, the needy and the helpless. The Federal Government will still subsidize 95 million meals every day. That's one out of seven of all the meals served in America. Head Start, senior nutrition programs, and child welfare programs will not be cut from the levels we proposed last year. More than one-half billion dollars has been proposed for minority business assistance. And research at the National Institutes of Health will be increased by over $100 million. While meeting all these needs, we intend to plug unwarranted tax loopholes and strengthen the law which requires all large corporations to pay a minimum tax.

I am confident the economic program we've put into operation will protect the needy while it triggers a recovery that will benefit all Americans. It will stimulate the economy, result in increased savings and provide capital for expansion, mortgages for home building and jobs for the unemployed.

Now that the essentials of that program are in place, our next major undertaking must be a program just as bold, just as innovative to make government again accountable to the people, to make our system of federalism work again.

Our citizens feel they've lost control of even the most basic decisions made about the essential services of government, such as schools, welfare, roads and even garbage collection. And they're right.

A maze of interlocking jurisdictions and levels of government confronts average citizens in trying to solve even the simplest of problems. They don't know where to turn for answers, who to hold accountable, who to praise, who to blame, who to vote for or against.

The main reason for this is the overpowering growth of Federal grants-in-aid programs during the past few decades.

In 1960, the Federal Government had 132 categorical grant programs, costing $7 billion. When I took office, there were approximately 500, costing nearly $100 billion -- 13 programs for energy, 36 for pollution control, 66 for social services, 90 for education. And here in the Congress, it takes at least 166 committees just to try to keep track of them.

You know and I know that neither the President nor the Congress can properly oversee this jungle of grants-in-aid; indeed, the growth of these grants had led to the distortion in the vital functions of government. As one Democratic Governor put it recently: "The national government should be worrying about arms control not potholes." The growth in these Federal programs has in the words of one intergovernmental commission made the Federal Government "more pervasive, more intrusive, more unmanageable, more ineffective and costly, and above all more unaccountable."

Well, let's solve this problem with a single, bold stroke, the return of some $47 billion in Federal programs to state and local government, together with the means to finance them and a transition period of nearly 10 years to avoid unnecessary disruption.

I will shortly send this Congress a message describing this program. I want to emphasize, however, that its full details will have been worked out only after close consultation with Congressional, state and local officials.

Now let me also note that private American groups have taken the lead in making Jan. 30 a day of solidarity with the people of Poland so, too, the European Parliament has called for March 21 to be an international day of support for Afghanistan. Well, I urge all peace-loving peoples to join together on those days, to raise their voices, to speak and pray for freedom.

Meanwhile, we're working for reduction of arms and military activities. As I announced in my address to the nation last Nov. 18, we have proposed to the Soviet Union a far-reaching agenda for mutual reduction of military forces and have already initiated negotiations with them in Geneva on intermediate-range nuclear forces.

In those talks it is essential that we negotiate from a position of strength. There must be a real incentive for the Soviets to take these talks seriously. This requires that we rebuild our defenses.

In the last decade, while we sought the moderation of Soviet power through a process of restraint and accommodation, the Soviets engaged in an unrelenting buildup of their military forces.

The protection of our national security has required that we undertake a substantial program to enhance our military forces.

We have not neglected to strengthen our traditional alliances in Europe and Asia, or to develop key relationships with our partners in the Middle East and other countries.

Building a more peaceful world requires a sound strategy and the national resolve to back it up. When radical forces threaten our friends, when economic misfortune creates conditions of instability, when strategically vital parts of the world fall under the shadow of Soviet power, our response can make the difference between peaceful change or disorder and violence. That's why we've laid such stress not only on our own defense, but on our vital foreign assistance program. Your recent passage of the foreign assistance act sent a signal to the world that America will not shrink from making the investments necessary for both peace and security. Our foreign policy must be rooted in realism, not naiveté or self-delusion.

A recognition of what the Soviet empire is about is the starting point. Winston Churchill, in negotiating with the Soviets, observed that they respect only strength and resolve in their dealings with other nations.

That's why we've moved to reconstruct our national defenses. We intend to keep the peace; we will also keep our freedom.

We have made pledges of a new frankness in our public statements and worldwide broadcasts. In the face of a climate of falsehood and misinformation, we've promised the world a season of truth, the truth of our great civilized ideas: individual liberty, representative government, the rule of law under God.

We've never needed walls, or mine fields or barbwire to keep our people in. Nor do we declare martial law to keep our people from voting for the kind of government they want.

Yes, we have our problems; yes, we're in a time of recession. And it's true, there's no quick fix, as I said, to instantly end the tragic pain of unemployment. But we will end it; the process has already begun and we'll see its effect as the year goes on.

We speak with pride and admiration of that little band of Americans who overcame insuperable odds to set this nation on course 200 years ago. But our glory didn't end with them. Americans ever since have emulated their deeds.

We don't have to turn to our history books for heroes. They're all around us. One who sits among you here tonight epitomized that heroism at the end of the longest imprisonment ever inflicted on men of our armed forces. Who will ever forget that night when we waited for television to bring us the scene of that first plane landing at Clark Field in the Philippines bringing our P.O.W.'s home? The plane door opened and Jeremiah Denton came slowly down the ramp. He caught sight of our flag, saluted it, said, "God bless America," and then thanked us for bringing him home.

Just two weeks ago, in the midst of a terrible tragedy on the Potomac, we saw again the spirit of American heroism at its finest, the heroism of dedicated rescue workers saving crash victims from icy waters.

And we saw the heroism of one of our young government employees, Lenny Skutnik, who, when he saw a woman lose her grip on the helicopter line, dived into the water and dragged her to safety.

And then there are countless quiet, everyday heroes of American life, parents who sacrifice long and hard so their children will know a better life than they've known; church and civic volunteers who help to feed, clothe, nurse and teach the needy; millions who've made our nation, and our nation's destiny, so very special unsung heroes who may not have realized their own dreams themselves but then who reinvest those dreams in their children.

Don't let anyone tell you that America's best days are behind her, that the American spirit has been vanquished. We've seen it triumph too often in our lives to stop believing in it now.

A hundred and twenty years ago the greatest of all our Presidents delivered his second State of the Union Message in this chamber. "We cannot escape history," Abraham Lincoln warned. "We of this Congress and this Administration will be remembered in spite of ourselves." The "trial through which we pass will light us down in honor or dishonor to the latest generation."

Well, that President and that Congress did not fail the American people. Together, they weathered the storm and preserved the union.

Let it be said of us that we, too, did not fail; that we, too, worked together to bring America through difficult times. Let us so conduct ourselves that two centuries from now, another Congress and another President, meeting in this chamber as we're meeting, will speak of us with pride, saying that we met the test and preserved for them in their day the sacred flame of liberty this last, best hope of man on Earth.

The Agenda is Victory

February 26, 1982
9th Annual CPAC Conference

Mr. Toastmaster [Representative] Mickey Edwards, thank you very much for those generous words, reverend clergy, ladies and gentlemen, we're delighted to be here at the ninth annual Conservative Political Action Conference.

Anyone looking at the exciting program you've scheduled over these four days, and the size of this gathering here tonight, can't help but be impressed with the energy and vitality of the conservative movement in America. We owe a special debt of gratitude to the staffs of American Conservative Union, Young Americans for Freedom, Human Events and National Review for making this year's conference the most successful in the brief but impressive history of this event.

Now, you may remember that when I spoke to you last year, I said the election victory we enjoyed in November of 1980 was not a victory of politics so much as it was a victory of ideas; not a victory for any one man or party, but a victory for a set of principles, principles that had been protected and nourished during the years of grim and heartbreaking defeats by a few dedicated Americans. Well, you are those Americans, and I salute you.

I've also come here tonight to remind you of how much remains to be done, and to ask your help in turning into reality even more of our hopes for America and the world. The agenda for this conference is victory, victory in this year's crucial congressional, state, and local elections.

The media coverage that you've received this week, the attention paid to you by so many distinguished Americans in and out of government -- conservative and not so conservative -- are testimony to the sea change that you've already brought about in American politics. But, despite the glitter of nights like this and the excitement we all still feel at the thought of enacting reforms we were only able to talk about a few years ago, we should always remember that our strength still lies in our faith in the good sense of the American people. And that the climate in Washington is still opposed to those enduring values, those "permanent things" that we've always believed in.

But Washington's fascination with passing trends and one-day headlines can sometimes cause serious problems over in the West Wing of the White House -- they cause them. There's the problem of leaks. Before we even announced the giveaway of surplus cheese, the warehouse mice had hired a lobbyist. [Laughter] And then a few weeks ago, those stories broke about the Kennedy tapes. And that caused something of a stir. Al Haig came in to brief me on his trip to Europe. I uncapped my pen, and he stopped talking. [Laughter] Up on the hill, I understand they were saying, "You need eloquence in the State Dining Room, wit in the East Room, and sign language in the Oval Office." [Laughter] It got so bad that I found myself telling every visitor there were absolutely no tape recordings being made. And if they wanted a transcript of that remark, just mention it to the potted plant on their way out. [Laughter]

But Washington is a place of fads and one-week stories. It's also a company town, and the company's name is government, big government. Now, I have a sneaking suspicion that a few of you might have agreed when we decided not to ask Congress for higher taxes. And I hope you realize it's going to take more than 402 days to completely change what's been going on for 40 years. I realized that the other day when I read a story about a private citizen in Louisiana who asked the government for help in developing his property. And he got back a letter that said: "We have observed that you have not traced the title prior to 1803. Before the final approval, it will be necessary that the title be traced previous to that year." Well, the citizen's answer was eloquent.

"Gentlemen," he wrote, "I am unaware that any educated man failed to know that Louisiana was purchased from France in 1803. The title of the land was acquired by France by the right of conquest from Spain. The land came in the possession of Spain in 1492 by the discovery by an Italian sailor, Christopher Columbus. The good Queen Isabella took the precaution of receiving the blessing of the Pope. ... The Pope is emissary of the Son of God, who made the world. Therefore, I believe that it is safe to assume that He also made that part of the United States called Louisiana. And I hope to hell you're satisfied." [Laughter]

Now, changing the habits of four decades is, as I say, going to take more than 402 days. But change will come if we conservatives are in this for the long haul -- if we owe our first loyalty to the ideas and principles we discussed, debated, developed, and popularized over the years. Last year I pointed to these principles as the real source of our strength as a political movement, and mentioned some of the intellectual giants who fostered and developed them -- men like

Frank Meyer, who reminded us that the robust individualism of America was part of deeper currents in Western civilization, currents that dictated respect for the law and the careful preservation of our political traditions.

Only a short time ago, conservatives filled this very room for a testimonial dinner to a great conservative intellect and scholar, author of the "The Conservative Mind," Russell Kirk. In a recent speech, Dr. Kirk has offered some political advice for the upcoming elections. He said now, more than ever, we must seek out the "gift of audacity." We must not become too comfortable with our new-found status in Washington. "When the walls of order are breached, the vigorous conservative must exclaim: Arm me, audacity, from head to foot." It was Napoleon, master of the huge battalions, who once said: "It is imagination that rules the human races"; and Disraeli who mentioned that "success is the child of audacity."

We must approach the upcoming elections with a forthright and direct message for the American people. We must remind them of the economic catastrophe that we faced on January 20th, 1981: millions out of work, inflation in double digits for two years in a row, interest rates hovering at 21 1/2 percent, productivity and the rate of growth in the gross national product down for the third year in a row, the money supply increasing by 12 percent -- and all this due to one overriding cause: Government was too big and had spent too much money.

Federal spending, in the last decade, went up more than 300 percent. In 1980 alone, it increased by 17 percent. Almost three-quarters of the federal budget was routinely referred to as "uncontrollable," largely due to increases in programs like food stamps, which in 15 years had increased by 16,000 percent, or Medicare and Medicaid -- up by more than 500 percent in just 10 years. Our national debt was approaching $1 trillion, and we were paying nearly $100 billion a year in interest on that debt -- more than enough money to run the federal government only 20 years ago.

In an effort to keep pace, taxes had increased by 220 percent in just 10 years, and we were looking at a tax increase from 1980 to 1984, already passed before we got here, of more than $300 billion. Unless we stop the spending juggernaut and reverse the trend toward even higher taxes, government by 1984 would be taking nearly one-quarter of the gross national product. Inflation and interest rates, according to several studies, would be heading toward 25 percent -- levels that would stifle enterprise and initiative and plunge the nation into even deeper economic crisis.

At this point last year, much of the smart money in Washington was betting, as it is today, on the failure of our proposals for restoring the economy, that we could never assemble the votes we needed to get our program for economic recovery through the Congress. But assemble the votes we did. For the first time in nearly 25 years, we slowed the spending juggernaut and got the taxpayers out from under the federal steamroller. We cut the rate of growth in federal spending almost in half. We lowered inflation to a single-digit rate, and it's still going down. It was 8.9 percent for all of 1981, but our January figure, at an annualized rate, is only 3 1/2 percent.

When they talk of what should be done for the poor, well, one thing alone, by reducing inflation, we increased the purchasing power of poor families by more than $250. We cut taxes for business and individuals and indexed to inflation. This last step ended once and for all that hidden profit on inflation that had made the federal bureaucracy America's largest growth industry.

We've moved against waste and fraud with a task force including our Inspectors General, who have already found thousands of people who've been dead for as long as seven years still receiving benefit checks from the government. We've concentrated on criminal prosecutions, and we've cut back in other areas like the multitude of films, pamphlets, and public relations experts, or, as we sometimes call them, the federal flood of flicks and flacks and foldouts.

We're cutting the size of the federal payroll by 75,000 over the next few years and are fighting to dismantle the Department of Energy and the Department of Education, agencies whose policies have frequently been exactly the opposite of what we need for real energy growth and sound education for our children.

Even now, less than five months after our program took full effect, we've seen the first signs of recovery. In January, leading economic indicators like housing permits showed an upturn. By 1983 we will begin bringing down the percentage of the gross national product consumed by both the federal deficit and by federal spending and taxes.

Our situation now is in some ways similar to that which confronted the United States and other Western nations shortly after World War II. Many economists then were predicting a return to depression once the stimulus of wartime spending was ended. But people were weary of wartime government controls, and here and in other nations like West Germany those controls were eliminated against the advice of some experts. At first, there was a period of hardship -- higher unemployment and declining growth. In fact, in 1946, our gross national product dropped 15 percent, but by 1947, the next year, it was holding steady and in 1948 increased by four percent. Unemployment began a steady decline. And in 1949 consumer prices were decreasing. A lot of the experts underestimated the economic growth that occurs once government stops meddling and the people take over. Well, they were wrong then, and they're wrong now.

The job of this administration and of the Congress is to move forward with additional cuts in the growth of federal spending and thereby ensure America's economic recovery. We have proposed budget cuts for 1983, and our proposals have met with cries of anguish. And those who utter the cries are equally anguished because there will be a budget deficit. They're a little like a dog sitting on a sharp rock howling with pain, when all he has to do is get up and move.

On the spending cuts now before the Congress and those tax reductions we've already passed for the American people, let me state we're standing by our program. We will not turn back or sound retreat.

You know, if I could just interject here, some of those people who say we must change direction when we've only been on this new direction for five months -- and it's only the first limited phase of the whole program -- it was described pretty well by Mickey Edwards, sitting right here, while we were having dinner. He said, "If you were sliding downhill on a snowy hill, and you know there's a cliff down there ahead of you at the bottom and suddenly there's a road that turns off to the right," he said, "you don't know where that road to the right goes, but," he says, "you take it." We know where that other one goes.

In the discussion of federal spending, the time has come to put to rest the sob sister attempts to portray our desire to get government spending under control as a hard-hearted attack on the poor people of America. In the first place, even with the economies that we've proposed, spending for entitlements -- benefits paid directly to individuals -- will actually increase by one-third over the next five years. And in 1983 non-defense items will amount to more than 70 percent of total spending.

As Dave Stockman pointed out the other day, we're still subsidizing 95 million meals a day, providing $70 billion in health care to the elderly and poor, some 47 million people. Some 10 million or more are living in subsidized housing. And we're still providing scholarships for a million and a half students. Only here in this city of Oz would a budget this big and this generous be characterized as a miserly attack on the poor.

Now, where do some of these attacks originate? They're coming from the very people whose past policies, all done in the name of compassion, brought us the current recession. Their policies drove up inflation and interest rates, and their policies stifled incentive, creativity, and halted the movement of the poor up the economic ladder. Some of their criticism is perfectly sincere. But let's also understand that some of their criticism comes from those who have a vested interest in a permanent welfare constituency and in government programs that reinforce the dependency of our people.

Well, I would suggest that no one should have a vested interest in poverty or dependency, that these tragedies must never be looked at as a source of votes for politicians or paychecks for bureaucrats. They are blights on our society that we must work to eliminate, not institutionalize.

Now, there are those who will always require help from the rest of us on a permanent basis, and we'll provide that help. To those with temporary need, we should have programs that are aimed at making them self-sufficient as soon as possible. How can limited government and fiscal restraint be equated with lack of compassion for the poor? How can a tax break that puts a little more money in the weekly paychecks of working people be seen as an attack on the needy?

Since when do we in America believe that our society is made up of two diametrically opposed classes -- one rich, one poor -- both in a permanent state of conflict and neither able to get ahead except at the expense of the other? Since when do we in America accept this alien and discredited theory of social and class warfare? Since when do we in America endorse the politics of envy and division?

When we reformed the welfare system in California and got the cheaters and the undeserving off the welfare rolls, instead of hurting the poor we were able to increase their benefits by more than 40 percent. By reducing the cost of government, we can continue bringing down inflation, the cruelest of all economic exploitations of the poor and the elderly. And by getting the economy moving again, we can create a vastly expanded job market that will offer the poor a way out of permanent dependency.

One man who held this office, a president vastly underrated by history, Calvin Coolidge, pointed out that a nation that is united in its belief in the work ethic and its desire for commercial success and economic progress is usually a healthy nation, a nation where it is easier to pursue the higher things in life like the development of science, the cultivation of the arts, the exploration of the great truths of religion and higher learning.

In arguing for economy in government, President Coolidge spoke of the burden of excessive government. He said: "I favor a policy of economy, not because I wish to save money, but because I wish to save people. The men and women of this country who toil are the ones who bear the cost of the government. Every dollar that we save means that their life will be so much the more abundant. Economy is idealism in its most practical form." And this is the message we conservatives can bring to the American people about our economic program. Higher productivity, a larger gross national product, a healthy Dow Jones average -- they are our goals and are worthy ones.

But our real concerns are not statistical goals or material gain. We want to expand personal freedom, to renew the American dream for every American. We seek to restore opportunity and reward, to value again personal achievement and individual excellence. We seek to rely on the ingenuity and energy of the American people to better their own lives and those of millions of others around the world.

We can be proud of the fact that a conservative administration has pursued these goals by confronting the nation's economic problems head-on. At the same time, we dealt with one other less publicized but equally grave problem: the serious state of disrepair in our national defenses.

The last Democratic administration had increased real defense spending at a rate of 3.3 percent a year. You know how much inflation was, so they were actually losing ground. By 1980 we had fighter planes that couldn't fly, Navy ships that couldn't leave port, a Rapid Deployment Force that was neither rapid nor deployable and not much of a force.

The protection of this nation's security is the most solemn duty of any president, and that's why I've asked for substantial increases in our defense budget -- substantial, but not excessive.

In 1962, President Kennedy's defense budget amounted to 44 percent of the entire budget. Ours is only 29 percent. In 1962, President Kennedy's request for military spending was 8.6 percent of the gross national product. Ours is only 6.3 percent. The Soviet Union outspends us on defense by 50 percent, an amount equal to 15 percent of their gross national product. During the campaign I was asked any number of times: If I were faced with a choice of balancing the budget or restoring our national defenses, what would I do? Every time I said, "Restore our defenses." And every time I was applauded.

So, let me be very clear. We will press for further cuts in federal spending. We will protect the tax reductions already passed. We will spend on defense what is necessary for our national security. I have no intention of leading the Republican Party into next fall's election on a platform of higher taxes and cut-rate defense. If our opponents want to go to the American people next fall and say, "We're the party that tried to cut spending, we're the party that tried to take away your tax cuts, we're the party that wanted a bargain-basement military and held a fire sale on national security," let's give them all the running room they want.

There are other matters on the political agenda for this coming year, matters I know that you've been discussing during the course of this conference. I hope one of them will be our attempt to give government back to the people. One hundred and thirty-two federal grants-in-aid in 1960 have grown to over 500 in 1981. Our federalism proposal would return the bulk of these programs to state and local governments, where they can be made more responsive to the people.

We're deeply committed to this program, because it has its roots in deep conservative principles. We've talked a long time about revitalizing our system of federalism. Now, with a single, bold stroke, we can restore the vigor and health of our state and local governments. This proposal lies at the heart of our legislative agenda for the next year, and we'll need your active support in getting it passed.

There are other issues before us. This administration is unalterably opposed to the forced busing of school children, just as we also support constitutional protection for the right of prayer in our schools. And there is the matter of abortion. We must with calmness and resolve help the vast majority of our fellow Americans understand that the more than one and a half a million abortions performed in America in 1980 amount to a great moral evil, an assault on the sacredness of human life.

And, finally, there's the problem of crime, a problem whose gravity cannot be underestimated. This administration has moved in its appointments to the federal bench and in its legislative proposals for bail and parole reform to assist in the battle against the lawless. But we must always remember that our legal system does not need reform so much as it needs transformation. And this cannot occur at just the federal level. It can really occur only when a society as a whole acknowledges principles that lie at the heart of modern conservatism. Right and wrong matters, individuals are responsible for their actions. Society has a right to be protected from those who prey on the innocent.

This, then, is the political agenda before us. Perhaps more than any group, your grassroots leadership, your candidate recruitment and training programs, your long years of hard work and dedication have brought us to this point and made this agenda possible.

We live today in a time of climactic struggle for the human spirit, a time that will tell whether the great civilized ideas of individual liberty, representative government, and the rule of law under God will perish or endure.

Whittaker Chambers, who sought idealism in Communism and found only disillusionment, wrote very movingly of his moment of awakening. It was at breakfast, and he was looking at the delicate ear of his tiny baby daughter, and he said that, suddenly, looking at that, he knew that couldn't just be an accident of nature. He said, while he didn't realize it at the time, he knows now that in that moment God had touched his forehead with His finger.

And later he wrote: "For in this century, within the next decades, will be decided for generations whether all mankind is to become Communist, whether the whole world is to become free, or whether in the struggle civilization as we know it is to be completely destroyed or completely changed. It is our fate to live upon that turning point in history." We've already come a long way together. Thank you for all that you've done for me, for the common values we cherish. Join me in a new effort, a new crusade.

Nostalgia has its time and place. Coming here tonight has been a sentimental journey for me, as I'm sure it has been for many of you. But nostalgia isn't enough. The challenge is now. It's time we stopped looking backward at how we got here.

We must ask ourselves tonight how we can forge and wield a popular majority from one end of this country to the other, a majority united on basic, positive goals with a platform broad enough and deep enough to endure long into the future, far beyond the lifespan of any single issue or personality.

We must reach out and appeal to the patriotic and fundamental ideals of average Americans who do not consider themselves "movement" people, but who respond to the same American ideals that we do. I'm not talking about some vague notion of an abstract, amorphous American mainstream. I'm talking about "Main Street" Americans in their millions. They come in all sizes, shapes and colors -- blue-collar workers, blacks, Hispanics, shopkeepers, scholars, service people, housewives, and professional men and women. They are the backbone of America, and we can't move America without moving their hearts and minds as well.

Fellow Americans, our duty is before us tonight. Let us go forward, determined to serve selflessly a vision of man with God, government for people, and humanity at peace. For it is now our task to tend and preserve, through the darkest and coldest nights, that "sacred fire of liberty" that President Washington spoke of two centuries ago, a fire that tonight remains a beacon to all the oppressed of the world, shining forth from this kindly, pleasant, greening land we call America.

God bless you, and thank you.

Defense and National Security

March 23, 1983

My fellow Americans, thank you for sharing your time with me tonight.

The subject I want to discuss with you, peace and national security, is both timely and important. Timely, because I've reached a decision which offers a new hope for our children in the 21st century, a decision I'll tell you about in a few minutes. And important because there's a very big decision that you must make for yourselves. This subject involves the most basic duty that any president and any people share, the duty to protect and strengthen the peace.

At the beginning of this year, I submitted to the Congress a defense budget which reflects my best judgment of the best understanding of the experts and specialists who advise me about what we and our allies must do to protect our people in the years ahead. That budget is much more than a long list of numbers, for behind all the numbers lies America's ability to prevent the greatest of human tragedies and preserve our free way of life in a sometimes dangerous world. It is part of a careful, long-term plan to make America strong again after too many years of neglect and mistakes.

Our efforts to rebuild America's defenses and strengthen the peace began 2 years ago when we requested a major increase in the defense program. Since then, the amount of those increases we first proposed has been reduced by half, through improvements in management and procurement and other savings.

The budget request that is now before the Congress has been trimmed to the limits of safety. Further deep cuts cannot be made without seriously endangering the security of the nation. The choice is up to the men and women you've elected to the Congress, and that means the choice is up to you.

Tonight, I want to explain to you what this defense debate is all about and why I'm convinced that the budget now before the Congress is necessary, responsible, and deserving of your support. And I want to offer hope for the future.

But first, let me say what the defense debate is not about. It is not about spending arithmetic. I know that in the last few weeks you've been bombarded with numbers and percentages. Some say we need only a 5-percent increase in defense spending. The so-called alternate budget backed by liberals in the House of Representatives would lower the figure to 2 to 3 percent, cutting our defense spending by $163 billion over the next 5 years. The trouble with all these numbers is that they tell us little about the kind of defense program America needs or the benefits and security and freedom that our defense effort buys for us.

What seems to have been lost in all this debate is the simple truth of how a defense budget is arrived at. It isn't done by deciding to spend a certain number of dollars. Those loud voices that are occasionally heard charging that the government is trying to solve a security problem by throwing money at it are nothing more than noise based on ignorance. We start by considering what must be done to maintain peace and review all the possible threats against our security. Then a strategy for strengthening peace and defending against those threats must be agreed upon. And, finally, our defense establishment must be evaluated to see what is necessary to protect against any or all of the potential threats. The cost of achieving these ends is totaled up, and the result is the budget for national defense.

There is no logical way that you can say, let's spend x billion dollars less. You can only say, which part of our defense measures do we believe we can do without and still have security against all contingencies? Anyone in the Congress who advocates a percentage or a specific dollar cut in defense spending should be made to say what part of our defenses he would eliminate, and he should be candid enough to acknowledge that his cuts mean cutting our commitments to allies or inviting greater risk or both.

The defense policy of the United States is based on a simple premise: The United States does not start fights. We will never be an aggressor. We maintain our strength in order to deter and defend against aggression—to preserve freedom and peace.

Since the dawn of the atomic age, we've sought to reduce the risk of war by maintaining a strong deterrent and by seeking genuine arms control. "Deterrence" means simply this: making sure any adversary who thinks about attacking the United States, or our allies, or our vital interests, concludes that the risks to him outweigh any potential gains. Once he understands that, he won't attack. We maintain the peace through our strength; weakness only invites aggression.

This strategy of deterrence has not changed. It still works. But what it takes to maintain deterrence has changed. It took one kind of military force to deter an attack when we had far more nuclear weapons than any other power; it takes another kind now that the

Soviets, for example, have enough accurate and powerful nuclear weapons to destroy virtually all of our missiles on the ground. Now, this is not to say that the Soviet Union is planning to make war on us. Nor do I believe a war is inevitable—quite the contrary. But what must be recognized is that our security is based on being prepared to meet all threats.

There was a time when we depended on coastal forts and artillery batteries, because, with the weaponry of that day, any attack would have had to come by sea. Well, this is a different world, and our defenses must be based on recognition and awareness of the weaponry possessed by other nations in the nuclear age.

We can't afford to believe that we will never be threatened. There have been two world wars in my lifetime. We didn't start them and, indeed, did everything we could to avoid being drawn into them. But we were ill-prepared for both. Had we been better prepared, peace might have been preserved.

For 20 years the Soviet Union has been accumulating enormous military might. They didn't stop when their forces exceeded all requirements of a legitimate defensive capability. And they haven't stopped now. During the past decade and a half, the Soviets have built up a massive arsenal of new strategic nuclear weapons— weapons that can strike directly at the United States.

As an example, the United States introduced its last new intercontinental ballistic missile, the Minute Man III, in 1969, and we're now dismantling our even older Titan missiles. But what has the Soviet Union done in these intervening years? Well, since 1969 the Soviet Union has built five new classes of ICBM's, and upgraded these eight times As a result, their missiles are much more powerful and accurate than they were several years ago, and they continue to develop more, while ours are increasingly obsolete.

The same thing has happened in other areas. Over the same period, the Soviet Union built 4 new classes of submarine-launched ballistic missiles and over 60 new missile submarines. We built 2 new types of submarine missiles and actually withdrew 10 submarines from strategic missions. The Soviet Union built over 200 new Backfire bombers, and their brand new Blackjack bomber is now under development. We haven't built a new long-range bomber since our B-52's were deployed about a quarter of a century ago, and we've already retired several hundred of those because of old age. Indeed, despite what many people think, our strategic forces only cost about 15 percent of the defense budget.

Another example of what's happened: in 1978 the Soviets had 600 intermediate range nuclear missiles based on land and were beginning to add the SS-20—a new, highly accurate, mobile missile with 3 warheads. We had none. Since then the Soviets have strengthened their lead. By the end of 1979, when Soviet leader Brezhnev declared "a balance now exists," the Soviets had over 800 warheads. We still had none. A year ago this month, Mr. Brezhnev pledged a moratorium, or freeze, on SS-20 deployment. But by last August, their 800 warheads had become more than 1,200. We still had none. Some freeze. At this time Soviet Defense Minister Ustinov announced "approximate parity of forces continues to exist." But the Soviets are still adding an average of 3 new warheads a week, and now have 1,300. These warheads can reach their targets in a matter of a few minutes. We still have none. So far, it seems that the Soviet definition of parity is a box score of 1,300 to nothing, in their favor.

So, together with our NATO allies, we decided in 1979 to deploy new weapons, beginning this year, as a deterrent to their SS-20's and as an incentive to the Soviet Union to meet us in serious arms control negotiations. We will begin that deployment late this year. At the same time, however, we're willing to cancel our program if the Soviets will dismantle theirs. This is what we've called a zero-zero plan. The Soviets are now at the negotiating table—and I think it's fair to say that without our planned deployments, they wouldn't be there.

Now let's consider conventional forces. Since 1974 the United States has produced 3,050 tactical combat aircraft. By contrast, the Soviet Union has produced twice as many. When we look at attack submarines, the United States has produced 27 while the Soviet Union has produced 61. For armored vehicles, including tanks, we have produced 11,200. The Soviet Union has produced 54,000—nearly 5 to 1 in their favor. Finally, with artillery, we've produced 950 artillery and rocket launchers while the Soviets have produced more than 13,000—a staggering 14-to-1 ratio.

There was a time when we were able to offset superior Soviet numbers with higher quality, but today they are building weapons as sophisticated and modern as our own.

As the Soviets have increased their military power, they've been emboldened to extend that power. They're spreading their military influence in ways that can directly challenge our vital interests and those of our allies.

The following aerial photographs, most of them secret until now, illustrate this point in a crucial area very close to home: Central America and the Caribbean Basin. They're not dramatic photographs. But I think they help give you a better understanding of what I'm talking about.

This Soviet intelligence collection facility, less than a hundred miles from our coast, is the largest of its kind in the world. The acres and acres of antennae fields and intelligence monitors are targeted on key U.S. military installations and sensitive activities. The installation in Lourdes, Cuba, is manned by 1,500 Soviet technicians. And the satellite ground station allows instant communications with Moscow. This 28 square-mile facility has grown by more than 60 percent in size and capability during the past decade.

In western Cuba, we see this military airfield and its complement of modern, Soviet-built Mig-23 aircraft. The Soviet Union uses this Cuban airfield for its own long-range reconnaissance missions. And earlier this month, two modern Soviet antisubmarine warfare aircraft began operating from it. During the past 2 years, the level of Soviet arms exports to Cuba can only be compared to the levels reached during the Cuban missile crisis 20 years ago.

This third photo, which is the only one in this series that has been previously made public, shows Soviet military hardware that has made its way to Central America. This airfield with its MI-8 helicopters, anti-aircraft guns, and protected fighter sites is one of a number of military facilities in Nicaragua which has received Soviet equipment funneled through Cuba, and reflects the massive military buildup going on in that country.

On the small island of Grenada, at the southern end of the Caribbean chain, the Cubans, with Soviet financing and backing, are in the process of building an airfield with a 10,000-foot runway. Grenada doesn't even have an air force. Who is it intended for? The

Caribbean is a very important passageway for our international commerce and military lines of communication. More than half of all American oil imports now pass through the Caribbean. The rapid buildup of Grenada's military potential is unrelated to any conceivable threat to this island country of under 110,000 people and totally at odds with the pattern of other eastern Caribbean States, most of which are unarmed.

The Soviet-Cuban militarization of Grenada, in short, can only be seen as power projection into the region. And it is in this important economic and strategic area that we're trying to help the governments of El Salvador, Costa Rica, Honduras, and others in their struggles for democracy against guerrillas supported through Cuba and Nicaragua.

These pictures only tell a small part of the story. I wish I could show you more without compromising our most sensitive intelligence sources and methods. But the Soviet Union is also supporting Cuban military forces in Angola and Ethiopia. They have bases in Ethiopia and South Yemen, near the Persian Gulf oil fields. They've taken over the port that we built at Cam Ranh Bay in Vietnam. And now for the first time in history, the Soviet Navy is a force to be reckoned with in the South Pacific.

Some people may still ask: Would the Soviets ever use their formidable military power? Well, again, can we afford to believe they won't? There is Afghanistan. And in Poland, the Soviets denied the will of the people and in so doing demonstrated to the world how their military power could also be used to intimidate.

The final fact is that the Soviet Union is acquiring what can only be considered an offensive military force. They have continued to build far more intercontinental ballistic missiles than they could possibly need simply to deter an attack. Their conventional forces are trained and equipped not so much to defend against an attack, as they are to permit sudden, surprise offensives of their own.

Our NATO allies have assumed a great defense burden, including the military draft in most countries. We're working with them and our other friends around the world to do more. Our defensive strategy means we need military forces that can move very quickly, forces that are trained and ready to respond to any emergency.

Every item in our defense program—our ships, our tanks, our planes, our funds for training and spare parts—is intended for one all-important purpose: to keep the peace. Unfortunately, a decade of neglecting our military forces had called into question our ability to do that.

When I took office in January 1981, I was appalled by what I found: American planes that couldn't fly and American ships that couldn't sail for lack of spare parts and trained personnel and insufficient fuel and ammunition for essential training. The inevitable result of all this was poor morale in our Armed Forces, difficulty in recruiting the brightest young Americans to wear the uniform, and difficulty in convincing our most experienced military personnel to stay on.

There was a real question then about how well we could meet a crisis. And it was obvious that we had to begin a major modernization program to ensure we could deter aggression and preserve the peace in the years ahead.

We had to move immediately to improve the basic readiness and staying power of our conventional forces, so they could meet—and therefore help deter—a crisis. We had to make up for lost years of investment by moving forward with a long-term plan to prepare our forces to counter the military capabilities our adversaries were developing for the future.

I know that all of you want peace, and so do I. I know too that many of you seriously believe that a nuclear freeze would further the cause of peace. But a freeze now would make us less, not more, secure and would raise, not reduce, the risks of war. It would be largely unverifiable and would seriously undercut our negotiations on arms reduction. It would reward the Soviets for their massive military buildup while preventing us from modernizing our aging and increasingly vulnerable forces. With their present margin of superiority, why should they agree to arms reductions knowing that we were prohibited from catching up?

Believe me, it wasn't pleasant for someone who had come to Washington determined to reduce government spending, but we had to move forward with the task of repairing our defenses or we would lose our ability to deter conflict now and in the future. We had to demonstrate to any adversary that aggression could not succeed, and that the only real solution was substantial, equitable, and effectively verifiable arms reduction—the kind we're working for right now in Geneva.

Thanks to your strong support, and bipartisan support from the Congress, we began to turn things around. Already, we're seeing some very encouraging results. Quality recruitment and retention are up dramatically—more high school graduates are choosing military careers, and more experienced career personnel are choosing to stay. Our men and women in uniform at last are getting the tools and training they need to do their jobs.

Ask around today, especially among our young people, and I think you will find a whole new attitude toward serving their country. This reflects more than just better pay, equipment, and leadership. You, the American people, have sent a signal to these young people that it is once again an honor to wear the uniform. That's not something you measure in a budget, but it's a very real part of our nation's strength.

It'll take us longer to build the kind of equipment we need to keep peace in the future, but we've made a good start.

We haven't built a new long-range bomber for 21 years. Now we're building the B-1. We hadn't launched one new strategic submarine for 17 years. Now we're building one Trident submarine a year. Our land-based missiles are increasingly threatened by the many huge, new Soviet ICBM's. We're determining how to solve that problem. At the same time, we're working in the START and INF negotiations with the goal of achieving deep reductions in the strategic and intermediate nuclear arsenals of both sides.

We have also begun the long-needed modernization of our conventional forces. The Army is getting its first new tank in 20 years. The Air Force is modernizing. We're rebuilding our Navy, which shrank from about a thousand ships in the late 1960's to 453 during the 1970's. Our nation needs a superior Navy to support our military forces and vital interests overseas. We're now on the road to achieving a 600-ship Navy and increasing the amphibious capabilities of our Marines, who are now serving the cause of peace in Lebanon. And we're building a real capability to assist our friends in the vitally important Indian Ocean and Persian Gulf region.

This adds up to a major effort, and it isn't cheap. It comes at a time when there are many other pressures on our budget and when the American people have already had to make major sacrifices during the recession. But we must not be misled by those who would make defense once again the scapegoat of the Federal budget.

The fact is that in the past few decades we have seen a dramatic shift in how we spend the taxpayer's dollar. Back in 1955, payments to individuals took up only about 20 percent of the Federal budget. For nearly three decades, these payments steadily increased and, this year, will account for 49 percent of the budget. By contrast, in 1955 defense took up more than half of the Federal budget. By 1980 this spending had fallen to a low of 23 percent. Even with the increase that I am requesting this year, defense will still amount to only 28 percent of the budget.

The calls for cutting back the defense budget come in nice, simple arithmetic. They're the same kind of talk that led the democracies to neglect their defenses in the 1930's and invited the tragedy of World War II. We must not let that grim chapter of history repeat itself through apathy or neglect.

This is why I'm speaking to you tonight to urge you to tell your Senators and Congressmen that you know we must continue to restore our military strength. If we stop in midstream, we will send a signal of decline, of lessened will, to friends and adversaries alike. Free people must voluntarily through open debate and democratic means, meet the challenge that totalitarians pose by compulsion. It's up to us, in our time, to choose and choose wisely between the hard but necessary task of preserving peace and freedom and the temptation to ignore our duty and blindly hope for the best while the enemies of freedom grow stronger day by day.

The solution is well within our grasp. But to reach it, there is simply no alternative but to continue this year, in this budget, to provide the resources we need to preserve the peace and guarantee our freedom.

Now, thus far tonight I've shared with you my thoughts on the problems of national security we must face together. My predecessors in the Oval Office have appeared before you on other occasions to describe the threat posed by Soviet power and have proposed steps to address that threat. But since the advent of nuclear weapons, those steps have been increasingly directed toward deterrence of aggression through the promise of retaliation.

This approach to stability through offensive threat has worked. We and our allies have succeeded in preventing nuclear war for more than three decades. In recent months, however, my advisers, including in particular the Joint Chiefs of Staff, have underscored the necessity to break out of a future that relies solely on offensive retaliation for our security.

Over the course of these discussions, I've become more and more deeply convinced that the human spirit must be capable of rising above dealing with other nations and human beings by threatening their existence. Feeling this way, I believe we must thoroughly examine every opportunity for reducing tensions and for introducing greater stability into the strategic calculus on both sides.

One of the most important contributions we can make is, of course, to lower the level of all arms, and particularly nuclear arms. We're engaged right now in several negotiations with the Soviet Union to bring about a mutual reduction of weapons. I will report to you a week from tomorrow my thoughts on that score. But let me just say, I'm totally committed to this course.

If the Soviet Union will join with us in our effort to achieve major arms reduction we will have succeeded in stabilizing the nuclear balance. Nevertheless, it will still be necessary to rely on the specter of retaliation, on mutual threat. And that's a sad commentary on the human condition. Wouldn't it be better to save lives than to avenge them? Are we not capable of demonstrating our peaceful intentions by applying all our abilities and our ingenuity to achieving a truly lasting stability? I think we are. Indeed, we must.

After careful consultation with my advisers, including the Joint Chiefs of Staff, I believe there is a way. Let me share with you a vision of the future which offers hope. It is that we embark on a program to counter the awesome Soviet missile threat with measures that are defensive. Let us turn to the very strengths in technology that spawned our great industrial base and that have given us the quality of life we enjoy today.

What if free people could live secure in the knowledge that their security did not rest upon the threat of instant U.S. retaliation to deter a Soviet attack, that we could intercept and destroy strategic ballistic missiles before they reached our own soil or that of our allies?

I know this is a formidable, technical task, one that may not be accomplished before the end of this century. Yet, current technology has attained a level of sophistication where it's reasonable for us to begin this effort. It will take years, probably decades of effort on many fronts. There will be failures and setbacks, just as there will be successes and breakthroughs. And as we proceed, we must remain constant in preserving the nuclear deterrent and maintaining a solid capability for flexible response. But isn't it worth every investment necessary to free the world from the threat of nuclear war? We know it is.

In the meantime, we will continue to pursue real reductions in nuclear arms, negotiating from a position of strength that can be ensured only by modernizing our strategic forces. At the same time, we must take steps to reduce the risk of a conventional military conflict escalating to nuclear war by improving our non-nuclear capabilities.

America does possess now the technologies to attain very significant improvements in the effectiveness of our conventional, nonnuclear forces. Proceeding boldly with these new technologies, we can significantly reduce any incentive that the Soviet Union may have to threaten attack against the United States or its allies.

As we pursue our goal of defensive technologies, we recognize that our allies rely upon our strategic offensive power to deter attacks against them. Their vital interests and ours are inextricably linked. Their safety and ours are one. And no change in technology can or will alter that reality. We must and shall continue to honor our commitments.

I clearly recognize that defensive systems have limitations and raise certain problems and ambiguities. If paired with offensive systems, they can be viewed as fostering an aggressive policy, and no one wants that. But with these considerations firmly in mind, I call upon the scientific community in our country, those who gave us nuclear weapons, to turn their great talents now to the cause of mankind and world peace, to give us the means of rendering these nuclear weapons impotent and obsolete.

Tonight, consistent with our obligations of the ABM treaty and recognizing the need for closer consultation with our allies, I'm taking an important first step. I am directing a comprehensive and intensive effort to define a long-term research and development program to begin to achieve our ultimate goal of eliminating the threat posed by strategic nuclear missiles. This could pave the way for arms control measures to eliminate the weapons themselves. We seek neither military superiority nor political advantage. Our only purpose—one all people share—is to search for ways to reduce the danger of nuclear war.

My fellow Americans, tonight we're launching an effort which holds the promise of changing the course of human history. There will be risks, and results take time. But I believe we can do it. As we cross this threshold, I ask for your prayers and your support.

Thank you, good night, and God bless you.

Address to National Religious Broadcasters

January 30, 1984

Thank you. Thank you very much. Thank you. Thank you, Brandt Gustavson, Dr. Ben Armstrong, and ladies and gentlemen, distinguished guests. Thank you all very much.

I'm going to depart from what I was going to say, or begin with here, for just a moment to tell a little story. And I hope Pat Boone won't mind. I'm going to tell it on him.

Some years ago when there was a subversive element that had moved into the motion picture industry and Hollywood, and there were great meetings that were held. There was one that was held in the Los Angeles Sports Arena. 16,000 people were there, and thousands of them up in the balcony were young people.

And Pat Boone stood up, and in speaking to this crowd he said, talking of communism, that he had daughters -- they were little girls then -- and he said, "I love them more than anything on Earth." "But," he said, "I would rather" -- and I thought, "I know what he's going to say and, oh, you must not say that." And yet I had underestimated him. He said, "I would rather that they die now believing in God than live to grow up under communism and die one day no longer believing in God."

There was a hushed moment, and then 16,000 people, all those thousands of young people came to their feet with a roar that you just -- it thrills you through and through.

Well, I thank you all very much. This is a moment I've been looking forward to. I remember with such pleasure the time we spent together last year. Today I feel like I'm doing more than returning for a speech; I -- I feel like I'm coming home.

Homecoming -- I think it is the proper word. Under this roof, some 4,000 of us are kindred spirits united by one burning belief: God is our Father; we are His children; together, brothers and sisters, we are one family.

Being family makes us willing to share the pain of problems we carry in our hearts. But families also come together in times of joy, and we can celebrate such a moment today. Hope is being reborn across this land by a mighty spiritual revival that's made you the miracle of the entire broadcasting industry.

I might say your success and my celebrating another birthday about this time of year are both a source of annoyance to a number of people.

Let me set the record straight on your account: The spectacular growth of CBN [Christian Broadcasting Network] and PTI [PTL - Praise the Lord] and Trinity [Trinity Broadcasting Network], of organizations that produce religious programs for radio and television, not to mention the booming industry in Christian books, underlines a far-reaching change in our country.

Americans yearn to explore life's deepest truths. And to say their entertainment -- their idea of entertainment is sex and violence and crime is an insult to their goodness and intelligence. We are people who believe love can triumph over hate, creativity over destruction, and hope over despair. And that's why so many millions hunger for your product -- God's good news.

In his book, "The Secret Kingdom," Pat Robertson told us, "There can be peace; there can be plenty; there can be freedom. They will come the minute human beings accept the principles of the invisible world and begin to live by them in the visible world." More and more of us are trying to do this. George Gallup has detected a rising tide of interest and involvement in religion among all levels of society.

I was pleased last year to proclaim 1983 the Year of the Bible. But, you know, a group called the ACLU severely criticized me for doing that.

Well I wear their indictment like a badge of honor.

I believe I stand in pretty good company. Abraham Lincoln called the Bible "the best gift God has given to man." "But for it," he said, "we wouldn't know right from wrong." Like that image of George Washington kneeling in prayer in the snow at Valley Forge, Lincoln described a people who knew it was not enough to depend on their own courage and goodness; they must also look to God their Father and Preserver. And their faith to walk with Him and trust in His Word brought them the blessings of comfort, power, and peace that they sought.

The torch of their faith has been passed from generation to generation. "The grass withereth, the flower fadeth, but the word of our God shall stand forever."

More and more Americans believe that loving God in their hearts is the ultimate value. Last year, not only were Year of the Bible activities held in every State of the Union, but more than 25 States and 500 cities issued their own Year of the Bible proclamations. One schoolteacher, Mary Gibson, in New York raised 4,000 dollars to buy Bibles for working people in downtown Manhattan.

1983 was the year more of us read the Good Book. Can we make a resolution here today? -- that 1984 will be the year we put its great truths into action?

My experience in this office I hold has only deepened a belief I've held for many years: Within the covers of that single Book are all the answers to all the problems that face us today, if we'd only read and believe.

Let's begin at the beginning. God is the center of our lives; the human family stands at the center of society; and our greatest hope for the future is in the faces of our children. Seven thousand Poles recently came to the christening of Maria Victoria Walesa, daughter of Danuta and Lech Walesa, to express their belief that solidarity of the family remains the foundation of freedom.

God's most blessed gift to His family is the gift of life. He sent us the Prince of Peace as a babe in a manger. I've said that we must be cautious in claiming God is on our side. I think the real question we must answer is, are we on His side?

I know what I'm about to say now is controversial, but I have to say it. This nation cannot continue turning a blind eye and a deaf ear to the taking of some 4,000 unborn children's lives every day. That's one every 21 seconds. One every 21 seconds.

We cannot pretend that America is preserving her first and highest ideal, the belief that each life is sacred, when we've permitted the deaths of 15 million helpless innocents since the Roe versus Wade decision -- 15 million children who will never laugh, never sing, never know the joy of human love, will never strive to heal the sick or feed the poor or make peace among nations. Abortion has denied them the first and most basic of human rights. We are all infinitely poorer for their loss.

There's another grim truth we should face up to: Medical science doctors confirm that when the lives of the unborn are snuffed out, they often feel pain, pain that is long and agonizing.

This nation fought a terrible war so that black Americans would be guaranteed their God-given rights. Abraham Lincoln recognized that we could not survive as a free land when some could decide whether others should be free or slaves. Well today another question begs to be asked: How can we survive as a free nation when some decide that others are not fit to live and should be done away with?

I believe no challenge is more important to the character of America than restoring the right to life to all human beings. Without that right, no other rights have meaning. "Suffer the little children to come unto me, and forbid them not, for such is the kingdom of God."

I will continue to support every effort to restore that protection including the Hyde-Jepsen respect life bill. I've asked for your all-out commitment, for the mighty power of your prayers, so that together we can convince our fellow countrymen that America should, can, and will preserve God's greatest gift.

Let us encourage those among us who are trying to provide positive alternatives to abortion -- groups like Mom's House, House of His Creation in Pennsylvania, Jim McKee's Sav-A-Life in Texas, which I mentioned to you last year. Begun as a response to the call of a conscience, Sav-A-Life has become a crisis counseling center and saved 22 children since it was founded in 1981.

I think we're making progress in upholding the sanctity of life of infants born with physical or mental handicaps. The Department of Health and Human Services has now published final regulations to address cases such as Baby Doe in Bloomington. That child was denied lifesaving surgery and starved to death because he had Down's Syndrome and some people didn't think his life would be worth living.

Not too long ago I was privileged to meet in the Oval Office a charming little girl -- tiny little girl -- filled with the joy of living. She was on crutches, but she swims; she rides horseback, and her smile steals your heart. She was born with the same defects as those Baby Does who have been denied the right to life. To see her, to see the love on the faces of her parents and their joy in her was the answer to this particular question.

Secretary Heckler and Surgeon General Koop deserve credit for designing regulations providing basic protections to the least among us. And the American Academy of Pediatrics and the National Association of Children's Hospitals have now affirmed a person's mental or physical handicap must not be the basis for deciding to withhold medical treatment.

Let me assure you of something else: We want parents to know their children will not be victims of child pornography. I look forward to signing a new bill now awaiting final action in a conference committee that will tighten our laws against child pornography. And we're concerned about enforcement of all the Federal antiobscenity laws.

Over the past year, the United States Customs Service has increased by 200 percent its confiscation of obscene materials coming in across our borders. We're also intensifying our drive against crimes of family violence and sexual abuse.

I happen to believe that protecting victims is just as important as safeguarding the rights of defendants.

Restoring the right to life and protecting people from violence and exploitation are important responsibilities. But as members of God's family we share another, and that is helping to build a foundation of faith and knowledge to prepare our children for the challenges of life. "Train up a child in the way he should go," Solomon wrote, "and when he is old he will not depart from it."

If we're to meet the challenge of educating for the space age, of opening eyes and minds to treasures of literature, music, and poetry, and of teaching values of faith, courage, responsibility, kindness, and love, then we must meet these challenges as one people. And parents must take the lead. And I believe they are.

I know one thing I'm sure most of us agree on: God, source of all knowledge, should never have been expelled from our children's classrooms. The great majority of our people support voluntary prayer in schools.

We hear of [cases] where courts say it is dangerous to allow students to meet in Bible study or prayer clubs. And then there was the case of that kindergarten class that was reciting a verse. They said, "We thank you for the flowers so sweet. We thank you for the food we eat. We thank you for the birds that sing. We thank you, God, for everything." A court order of -- a court of appeals ordered them to stop. They were supposedly violating the Constitution of the United States.

Well, Teddy Roosevelt told us, "The American people are slow to wrath, but when their wrath is once kindled, it burns like a consuming flame."

I think Americans are getting angry. I think they have a message, and Congress better listen. We are a government of, by, and for the people. And people want a constitutional amendment making it unequivocally clear our children can hold voluntary prayer in every school across this land. And if we could get God and discipline back in our schools, maybe we could get drugs and violence out.

I know that some believe that voluntary prayer in schools should be restricted to a moment of silence. We already have the right to remain silent -- we can take our fifth amendment.

Seriously, we need a new amendment to restore the rights that were taken from us. Senator Baker has assured us that he -- we will get a vote on our amendment. And with your help, we can win, and that will be a great victory for our children.

During the last decade, we've seen people's commitment to religious liberty expressed by the establishment of thousands of new religious schools. These schools were built by the sacrifices of parents determined to provide a quality education for their children in an environment that permits traditional values to flourish.

Now I believe that some of you've met with my advisers to discuss the situation of religious schools in Nebraska. We have all seen news accounts of the jailing of a minister, the padlocking of a church, and the continuing imprisonment of fathers of students. This issue of religious liberty has arisen in other States. The question is how to find a balance between assuring quality of education and preserving freedom for churches and parents who want their schools to reflect their faith.

These cases have mostly proceeded in State courts. A number of State supreme courts have reached decisions that moderated the effect of State regulations on religious schools. Last week, a panel appointed by the Governor of Nebraska concluded that the State's regulations violate the religious liberties of Christian schools.

I'm a firm believer in the separation of powers, that this nation is a federation of sovereign States. But isn't it time for the Nebraska courts or legislature to solve this problem by a speedy reconsideration? I hope -- I hope some way can be found to resolve the legal issues without having people in jail for doing what they think is right.

Within our families, neighborhoods, schools, and places of work, let us continue reaching out, renewing our spirit of friendship, community service, and caring for each other -- a spirit that flows like a deep and powerful river through the history of our nation.

I made a point last year which some of our critics jumped on, but I believe it has merit. Government bureaucracies spend billions for problems related to drugs, alcoholism, and disease. How much of that money could we save, how much better off might Americans be if all of us tried a little harder to live by the Ten Commandments and the Golden Rule? I've been told that since the beginning of civilization millions and millions of laws have been written. I've even heard someone suggest it was as many as several billion. And yet, taken all together, all those millions and millions of laws have not improved on the Ten Commandments one bit.

Look at projects like CBN's "Operation Blessing," Moody Bible Institute's "Open Line" radio program, inner city -- or the radio program, "Inner City," I should say, in Chicago, and the work of Dr. E.V. Hill of Mt. Zion Baptist Church in Los Angeles. They show us that America is more than just government on the one hand and helpless individuals on the other. They show us that lives are saved, people are reborn and, yes, dreams come true when we heed the voice of the Spirit, minister to the needy, and glorify God. That is the stuff of which miracles are made.

Our mission stretches far beyond our borders; God's family knows no borders. In your life you face daily trials, but millions of believers in other lands face far worse. They are mocked and persecuted for the crime of loving God. To every religious dissident trapped in that cold, cruel existence, we send our love and support. Our message? You are not alone; you are not forgotten; do not lose your faith and hope because someday you, too, will be free.

If the Lord -- If the Lord is our light, our strength, and our salvation, whom shall we fear? Of whom shall we be afraid? No matter where we live, we have a promise that can make all the difference, a promise from Jesus to soothe our sorrows, heal our hearts, and drive away our fears. He promised there will never be a dark night that does not end. Our "weeping may endure for a night, but joy cometh in the morning." He promised if our hearts are true, His love will be as sure as sunlight. And, by dying for us, Jesus showed how far our love should be ready to go: all the way.

"For God so loved the world that He gave His only begotten Son, that whosoever believeth in Him should not perish but have everlasting life."

I'm a little self-conscious because I know very well you all could recite that verse to me.

Helping each other, believing in Him, we need never be afraid. We will be part of something far more powerful, enduring, and good than all the forces here on Earth. We will be a part of paradise.

May God keep you always, and may you always keep God. Thank you very much.

40th Anniversary of D-Day

June 6, 1984
Omaha Beach, Normandy, France

We stand today at a place of battle, one that 40 years ago saw and felt the worst of war. Men bled and died here for a few feet of -- or inches of -- sand, as bullets and shellfire cut through their ranks. About them, General Omar Bradley later said, "Every man who set foot on Omaha Beach that day was a hero."

Some who survived the battle of June 6, 1944, are here today. Others who hoped to return never did.

"Someday, Lis, I'll go back," said Private First Class Peter Robert Zanatta, of the 37th Engineer Combat Battalion, and first assault wave to hit Omaha Beach. "I'll go back, and I'll see it all again. I'll see the beach, the barricades, and the graves."

Those words of Private Zanatta come to us from his daughter, Lisa Zanatta Henn, in a heart-rending story about the event her father spoke of so often. "In his words, the Normandy invasion would change his life forever," she said. She tells some of his stories of World War II but says of her father, "the story to end all stories was D-Day."

"He made me feel the fear of being on the boat waiting to land. I can smell the ocean and feel the seasickness. I can see the looks on his fellow soldiers' faces -- the fear, the anguish, the uncertainty of what lay ahead. And when they landed, I can feel the strength and courage of the men who took those first steps through the tide to what must have surely looked like instant death."

Private Zanatta's daughter wrote to me, "I don't know how or why I can feel this emptiness, this fear, or this determination, but I do. Maybe it's the bond I had with my father. All I know is that it brings tears to my eyes to think about my father as a 20-year-old boy having to face that beach."

The anniversary of D-Day was always special to her family. And like all the families of those who went to war, she describes how she came to realize her own father's survival was a miracle: "So many men died. I know that my father watched many of his friends be killed. I know that he must have died inside a little each time. But his explanation to me was, "You did what you had to do, and you kept on going.""

When men like Private Zanatta and all our Allied forces stormed the beaches of Normandy 40 years ago they came not as conquerors, but as liberators. When these troops swept across the French countryside and into the forests of Belgium and Luxembourg they came not to take, but to return what had been wrongfully seized. When our forces marched into Germany they came not to prey on a brave and defeated people, but to nurture the seeds of democracy among those who yearned to be free again.

We salute them today. But, Mr. President [Francois Mitterand of France], we also salute those who, like yourself, were already engaging the enemy inside your beloved country -- the French Resistance. Your valiant struggle for France did so much to cripple the enemy and spur the advance of the armies of liberation. The French Forces of the Interior will forever personify courage and national spirit. They will be a timeless inspiration to all who are free and to all who would be free.

Today, in their memory, and for all who fought here, we celebrate the triumph of democracy. We reaffirm the unity of democratic people who fought a war and then joined with the vanquished in a firm resolve to keep the peace.

From a terrible war we learned that unity made us invincible; now, in peace, that same unity makes us secure. We sought to bring all freedom-loving nations together in a community dedicated to the defense and preservation of our sacred values. Our alliance, forged in the crucible of war, tempered and shaped by the realities of the post-war world, has succeeded. In Europe, the threat has been contained, the peace has been kept.

Today, the living here assembled -- officials, veterans, citizens -- are a tribute to what was achieved here 40 years ago. This land is secure. We are free. These things are worth fighting and dying for.

Lisa Zanatta Henn began her story by quoting her father, who promised that he would return to Normandy. She ended with a promise to her father, who died 8 years ago of cancer: "I'm going there, Dad, and I'll see the beaches and the barricades and the monuments. I'll see the graves, and I'll put flowers there just like you wanted to do. I'll never forget what you went through, Dad, nor will I let any one else forget. And, Dad, I'll always be proud."

Through the words of his loving daughter, who is here with us today, a D-Day veteran has shown us the meaning of this day far better than any President can. It is enough to say about Private Zanatta and all the men of honor and courage who fought beside him four decades ago: We will always remember. We will always be proud. We will always be prepared, so we may always be free.

Creators of the Future

March 8, 1985

Thank you all very much. Thank you Vice Chairman [of the American Conservative Union James A.] Linen, for those very kind words. I'm grateful to the American Conservative Union, Young Americans for Freedom, National Review, Human Events, for organizing this wonderful evening. When you work in the White House, you don't get to see your old friends as much as you'd like. And I always see the Conservative Political Action Conference speech as my opportunity to "dance with the one that brung ya."

There's so much I want to talk about tonight. I've been thinking, in the weeks since the inauguration, that we are at an especially dramatic turning point in American history. And just putting it all together in my mind, I've been reviewing the elements that have led to this moment.

Ever since F.D.R. and the New Deal, the opposition party, and particularly those of a liberal persuasion, have dominated the political debate. Their ideas were new; they had momentum; they captured the imagination of the American people. The left held sway for a long time. There was a right, but it was, by the '40s and '50s, diffuse and scattered, without a unifying voice.

But in 1964 came a voice in the wilderness -- Barry Goldwater; the great Barry Goldwater, the first major party candidate of our time who was a true-blue, undiluted conservative. He spoke from principle, and he offered vision. Freedom -- he spoke of freedom: freedom from the government's increasing demands on the family purse, freedom from the government's increasing usurpation of individual rights and responsibilities, freedom from the leaders who told us the price of world peace is continued acquiescence to totalitarianism. He was ahead of his time. When he ran for president, he won six states and lost 44. But his candidacy worked as a precursor of things to come.

A new movement was stirring. And in the 1960's Young Americans for Freedom is born; National Review gains readership and prestige in the intellectual community; Human Events becomes a major voice on the cutting edge. In the '70s the anti-tax movement begins. Actually, it was much more than an anti-tax movement, just as the Boston Tea Party was much more than an anti-tax initiative. In the late '70s, Proposition 13 and the Sagebrush Rebellion; in 1980, for the first time in 28 years, a Republican Senate is elected; so, may I say, is a conservative president. In 1984, that conservative administration is reselected in a 49-state sweep. And the day the votes came in, I thought of Walt Whitman: "I hear America singing."

This great turn from left to right was not just a case of the pendulum swinging. First, the left hold sway and then the right, and here comes the left again. The truth is, conservative thought is no longer over here on the right; it's the mainstream now. And the tide of history is moving irresistibly in our direction. Why? Because the other side is virtually bankrupt of ideas. It has nothing more to say, nothing to add to the debate. It has spent its intellectual capital, such as it was, and it has done its deeds. Now, we're not in power because they failed to gain electoral support over the past 50 years. They did win support. And the result was chaos, weakness, and drift. Ultimately, though, their failures yielded one great thing -- us guys. We in this room are not simply profitting from their bankruptcy; we are where we are because we're winning the contest of ideas. In fact, in the past decade, all of a sudden, quietly, mysteriously, the Republican Party has become the party of ideas.

We became the party of the most brilliant and dynamic young minds. I remember them, just a few years ago, running around scrawling Laffer curves on table napkins, going to symposia and talking about how social programs did not eradicate poverty, but entrenched it; writing studies on why the latest weird and unnatural idea from the social engineers is weird and unnatural. You were there. They were your ideas, your symposia, your books, and usually somebody else's table napkins.

All of a sudden, Republicans were not defenders of the status quo but creators of the future. They were looking at tomorrow with all the single-mindedness of an inventor. In fact, they reminded me of the American inventors of the 19th and 20th centuries who filled the world with light and recorded sound.

The new conservatives made anew the connection between economic justice and economic growth. Growth in the economy would not only create jobs and paychecks, they said; it would enhance familial stability and encourage a healthy optimism about the future. Lower those tax rates, they said, and let the economy become the engine of our dreams. Pull back regulations, and encourage free and open competition. Let the men and women of the marketplace decide what they want.

But along with that, perhaps the greatest triumph of modern conservatism has been to stop allowing the left to put the average American on the moral defensive. By average American, I mean the good, decent, rambunctious, and creative people who raise the families, go to church, and help out when the local library holds a fund-raiser; people who have a stake in the community because they are the community.

These people had held true to certain beliefs and principles that for 20 years the intelligentsia were telling us were hopelessly out of date, utterly trite, and reactionary. You want prayer in the schools? How primitive, they said. You oppose abortion? How oppressive, how antimodern. The normal was portrayed as eccentric, and only the abnormal was worthy of emulation. The irreverent was celebrated, but only irreverence about certain things: irreverence toward, say, organized religion, yes; irreverence toward established liberalism, not too much of that. They celebrated their courage in taking on safe targets and patted each other on the back for slinging stones at a confused Goliath, who was too demoralized and really too good to fight back. But now one simply senses it. The American people are no longer on the defensive. I believe the conservative movement deserves some credit for this. You spoke for the permanent against the merely prevalent, and ultimately you prevailed.

I believe we conservatives have captured the moment, captured the imagination of the American people. And what now? What are we to do with our success? Well, right now, with conservative thought accepted as mainstream thought and with the people of our country leading the fight to freedom, now we must move.

You remember your Shakespeare: "There is a tide in the affairs of men which, taken at the flood, leads on to fortune. Omitted, all the voyage of their life is bound in shallows and in miseries. On such a full sea are we now afloat. And we must take the current when it serves, or lose our ventures." I spoke in the -- [applause]. It's typical, isn't it? I just quoted a great writer, but as an actor, I get the bow. [Laughter]

I spoke in the State of the Union of a second American revolution, and now is the time to launch that revolution and see that it takes hold. If we move decisively, these years will not be just a passing era of good feeling, not just a few good years, but a true golden age of freedom.

The moment is ours, and we must seize it. There's work to do. We must prolong and protect our growing prosperity so that it doesn't become just a passing phase, a natural adjustment between periods of recession. We must move further to provide incentives and make America the investment capital of the world.

We must institute a fair tax system and turn the current one on its ear. I believe there is natural support in our country for a simplified tax system, with still lower tax rates but a broader base, with everyone paying their fair share and no more. We must eliminate unproductive tax shelters. Again, there is natural support among Americans, because Americans are a fair-minded people.

We must institute enterprise zones and a lower youth minimum wage so we can revitalize distressed areas and teenagers can get jobs. We're going to take our revolution to the people, all of the people. We're going to go to black Americans and members of all minority groups, and we're going to make our case.

Part of being a revolutionary is knowing that you don't have to acquiesce to the tired, old ideas of the past. One such idea is that the opposition party has black America and minority America locked up, that they own black America. Well, let me tell you, they own nothing but the past. The old alignments are no longer legitimate, if they ever were.

We're going to reach out, and we need your help. Conservatives were brought up to hate deficits, and justifiably so. We've long thought there are two things in Washington that are unbalanced -- the budget and the liberals.

But we cannot reduce the deficit by raising taxes. And just so that every "i" is dotted and every "t" is crossed, let me repeat tonight for the benefit of those who never seem to get the message: we will not reduce the deficit by raising taxes. We need more taxes like John McLaughlin [Washington executive editor of National Review] needs assertiveness training.

Now, whether government borrows or increases taxes, it will be taking the same amount of money from the private economy, and either way, that's too much. We must bring down government spending. We need a constitutional amendment requiring a balanced budget. It's something that 49 states already require -- no reason the federal government should be any different.

We need the line-item veto, which 43 governors have -- no reason that the president shouldn't. And we have to cut waste. The Grace Commission has identified billions of dollars that are wasted and that we can save.

But the domestic side isn't the only area where we need your help. All of us in this room grew up, or came to adulthood, in a time when the doctrine of Marx and Lenin was coming to divide the world. Ultimately, it came to dominate remorselessly whole parts of it. The

Soviet attempt to give legitimacy to its tyranny is expressed in the infamous Brezhnev doctrine, which contends that once a country has fallen into Communist darkness, it can never again be allowed to see the light of freedom. Well, it occurs to me that history has already begun to repeal that doctrine. It started one day in Grenada. We only did our duty, as a responsible neighbor and a lover of peace, the day we went in and returned the government to the people and rescued our own students. We restored that island to liberty. Yes, it's only a small island, but that's what the world is made of -- small islands yearning for freedom.

There's much more to do. Throughout the world the Soviet Union and its agents, client states, and satellites are on the defensive -- on the moral defensive, the intellectual defensive, and the political and economic defensive. Freedom movements arise and assert themselves. They're doing so on almost every continent populated by man -- in the hills of Afghanistan, in Angola, in Kampuchea, in Central America. In making mention of freedom fighters, all of us are privileged to have in our midst tonight one of the brave commanders who lead the Afghan freedom fighters -- Abdul Haq. Abdul Haq, we are with you.

They are our brothers, these freedom fighters, and we owe them our help. I've spoken recently of the freedom fighters of Nicaragua. You know the truth about them. You know who they're fighting and why. They are the moral equal of our Founding Fathers and the brave men and women of the French Resistance. We cannot turn away from them, for the struggle here is not right versus left; it is right versus wrong.

Now I am against sending troops to Central America. They are simply not needed. Given a chance and the resources the people of the area can fight their own fight. They have the men and women. They're capable of doing it. They have the people of their country behind them. All they need is our support. All they need is proof that we care as much about the fight for freedom 700 miles from our shores as the Soviets care about the fight against freedom 5,000 miles from theirs. And they need to know that the U.S. supports them with more than just pretty words and good wishes. We need your help on this and I mean each of you -- involved active strong and vocal. And we need more.

All of you know that we're researching nonnuclear technologies that may enable us to prevent nuclear ballistic missiles from reaching U.S. soil or that of our allies. I happen to believe -- logic forces me to believe -- that this new defense system th,e Strategic Defense Initiative, is the most hopeful possibility of our time. Its primary virtue is clear. If anyone ever attacked us Strategic Defense would be there to protect us. It could conceivably save millions of lives.

SDI has been criticized on the grounds that it might upset any chance of an arms control agreement with the Soviets. But SDI is arms control. If SDI is, say, 80 percent effective, then it will make any Soviet attack folly. Even partial success in SDI would strengthen deterrence and keep the peace. And if our SDI research is successful the prospects for real reduction in U.S. and Soviet offensive nuclear forces will be greatly enhanced.

It is said that SDI would deal a blow to the so-called East-West balance of power. Well let's think about that. The Soviets already are investing roughly as much on strategic defenses as they are on their offensive nuclear forces. This could quickly tip the East-West balance if we had no defense of our own. Would a situation of comparable defenses threaten us? No, for we're not planning on being the first to use force. As we strive for our goal of eventual elimination of nuclear weapons, each side would retain a certain amount of defensive -- or of, I should say, destructive power -- a certain number of missiles. But it would not be in our interest, or theirs, to build more and more of them.

Now, one would think our critics on the left would quickly embrace, or at least be open-minded about a system that promises to reduce the size of nuclear missile forces on both sides and to greatly enhance the prospects for real arms reductions. And yet we hear SDI belittled by some with nicknames, or demagogued with charges that it will bring war to the heavens.

They complain that it won't work, which is odd from people who profess to believe in the perfectibility of man-machines after all. And man-machines are so much easier to manipulate. They say it won't be 100 percent effective, which is odd, since they don't ask for 100 percent effectiveness in their social experiments. They say SDI is only in the research stage and won't be realized in time to change things. To which, as I said last month, the only reply is: then let's get started.

Now, my point here is not to question the motives of others. But it's difficult to understand how critics can object to exploring the possibility of moving away from exclusive reliance upon nuclear weapons. The truth is, I believe that they find it difficult to embrace any idea that breaks with the past, that breaks with consensus thinking and the common establishment wisdom. In short, they find it difficult and frightening to alter the status quo.

And what are we to do when these so-called opinion leaders of an outworn philosophy are out there on television and in the newspapers with their steady drumbeat of doubt and distaste? Well, when all you have to do to win is rely on the good judgment of the American people, then you're in good shape, because the American people have good judgment. I know it isn't becoming of me, but I like to think that maybe 49 of our 50 states displayed that judgment just a few months ago.

What we have to do, all of us in this room, is get out there and talk about SDI. Explain it, debate it, tell the American people the facts. It may well be the most important work we do in the next few years. And if we try, we'll succeed. So, we have great work ahead of us, big work. But if we do it together and with complete commitment, we can change our country and history forever.

Once during the campaign, I said, "This is a wonderful time to be alive," and I meant that. I meant that we're lucky not to live in pale and timid times. We've been blessed with the opportunity to stand for something -- for liberty and freedom and fairness. And these are things worth fighting for, worth devoting our lives to. And we have good reason to be hopeful and optimistic.

We've made much progress already. So, let us go forth with good cheer and stout hearts -- happy warriors out to seize back a country and a world to freedom.

Thank you, and God bless you. Thank you very much.

Space Shuttle Challenger Address

January 28, 1986

Ladies and gentlemen, I'd planned to speak to you tonight to report on the state of the Union, but the events of earlier today have led me to change those plans. Today is a day for mourning and remembering. Nancy and I are pained to the core by the tragedy of the shuttle Challenger. We know we share this pain with all of the people of our country. This is truly a national loss.

Nineteen years ago, almost to the day, we lost three astronauts in a terrible accident on the ground. But we've never lost an astronaut in flight; we've never had a tragedy like this. And perhaps we've forgotten the courage it took for the crew of the shuttle. But they, the Challenger Seven, were aware of the dangers, but overcame them and did their jobs brilliantly. We mourn seven heroes: Michael Smith, Dick Scobee, Judith Resnik, Ronald McNair, Ellison Onizuka, Gregory Jarvis, and Christa McAuliffe. We mourn their loss as a nation together.

For the families of the seven, we cannot bear, as you do, the full impact of this tragedy. But we feel the loss, and we're thinking about you so very much. Your loved ones were daring and brave, and they had that special grace, that special spirit that says, "Give me a challenge, and I'll meet it with joy." They had a hunger to explore the universe and discover its truths. They wished to serve, and they did. They served all of us. We've grown used to wonders in this century. It's hard to dazzle us. But for 25 years the United States space program has been doing just that. We've grown used to the idea of space, and perhaps we forget that we've only just begun. We're still pioneers. They, the members of the Challenger crew, were pioneers.

And I want to say something to the schoolchildren of America who were watching the live coverage of the shuttle's takeoff. I know it is hard to understand, but sometimes painful things like this happen. It's all part of the process of exploration and discovery. It's all part of taking a chance and expanding man's horizons. The future doesn't belong to the fainthearted; it belongs to the brave. The Challenger crew was pulling us into the future, and we'll continue to follow them.

I've always had great faith in and respect for our space program, and what happened today does nothing to diminish it. We don't hide our space program. We don't keep secrets and cover things up. We do it all up front and in public. That's the way freedom is, and we wouldn't change it for a minute. We'll continue our quest in space. There will be more shuttle flights and more shuttle crews and, yes, more volunteers, more civilians, more teachers in space. Nothing ends here; our hopes and our journeys continue. I want to add that I wish I could talk to every man and woman who works for NASA or who worked on this mission and tell them: "Your dedication and professionalism have moved and impressed us for decades. And we know of your anguish. We share it."

There's a coincidence today. On this day 390 years ago, the great explorer Sir Francis Drake died aboard ship off the coast of Panama. In his lifetime the great frontiers were the oceans, and an historian later said, "He lived by the sea, died on it, and was buried in it." Well, today we can say of the Challenger crew: Their dedication was, like Drake's, complete.

The crew of the Space Shuttle Challenger honored us by the manner in which they lived their lives. We will never forget them, nor the last time we saw them, this morning, as they prepared for their journey and waved goodbye and "slipped the surly bonds of earth" to "touch the face of God."

Brandenburg Gate Address

June 12, 1987

Thank you very much. Chancellor Kohl, Governing Mayor Diepgen, ladies and gentlemen: Twenty-four years ago, President John F. Kennedy visited Berlin, speaking to the people of this city and the world at the city hall. Well, since then two other presidents have come, each in his turn, to Berlin. And today I, myself, make my second visit to your city.

We come to Berlin, we American Presidents, because it's our duty to speak, in this place, of freedom. But I must confess, we're drawn here by other things as well: by the feeling of history in this city, more than 500 years older than our own nation; by the beauty of the Grunewald and the Tiergarten; most of all, by your courage and determination. Perhaps the composer, Paul Lincke, understood something about American Presidents. You see, like so many Presidents before me, I come here today because wherever I go, whatever I do: "Ich hab noch einen koffer in Berlin." [I still have a suitcase in Berlin.]

Our gathering today is being broadcast throughout Western Europe and North America. I understand that it is being seen and heard as well in the East. To those listening throughout Eastern Europe, I extend my warmest greetings and the good will of the American people. To those listening in East Berlin, a special word: Although I cannot be with you, I address my remarks to you just as surely as to those standing here before me. For I join you, as I join your fellow countrymen in the West, in this firm, this unalterable belief: Es gibt nur ein Berlin. [There is only one Berlin.]

Behind me stands a wall that encircles the free sectors of this city, part of a vast system of barriers that divides the entire continent of Europe. From the Baltic, south, those barriers cut across Germany in a gash of barbed wire, concrete, dog runs, and guard towers. Farther south, there may be no visible, no obvious wall. But there remain armed guards and checkpoints all the same -- still a restriction on the right to travel, still an instrument to impose upon ordinary men and women the will of a totalitarian state. Yet it is here in Berlin where the wall emerges most clearly -- here, cutting across your city, where the news photo and the television screen have imprinted this brutal division of a continent upon the mind of the world. Standing before the Brandenburg Gate, every man is a German, separated from his fellow men. Every man is a Berliner, forced to look upon a scar.

President von Weizsacker has said: "The German question is open as long as the Brandenburg Gate is closed."

Today I say: As long as this gate is closed, as long as this scar of a wall is permitted to stand, it is not the German question alone that remains open, but the question of freedom for all mankind. Yet I do not come here to lament. For I find in Berlin a message of hope, even in the shadow of this wall, a message of triumph.

In this season of spring in 1945, the people of Berlin emerged from their air-raid shelters to find devastation thousands of miles away; the people of the United States reached out to help. And in 1947 Secretary of State -- as you've been told -- George Marshall announced the creation of what would become known as the Marshall plan. Speaking precisely 40 years ago this month, he said:

"Our policy is directed not against any country or doctrine, but against hunger, poverty, desperation, and chaos."

In the Reichstag a few moments ago, I saw a display commemorating this 40th anniversary of the Marshall plan. I was struck by the sign on a burnt-out, gutted structure that was being rebuilt. I understand that Berliners of my own generation can remember seeing signs like it dotted throughout the Western sectors of the city. The sign read simply: "The Marshall plan is helping here to strengthen the free world." A strong, free world in the West, that dream became real. Japan rose from ruin to become an economic giant. Italy, France, Belgium -- virtually every nation in Western Europe saw political and economic rebirth; the European Community was founded.

In West Germany and here in Berlin, there took place an economic miracle, the Wirtschaftswunder. Adenauer, Erhard, Reuter, and other leaders understood the practical importance of liberty -- that just as truth can flourish only when the journalist is given freedom of speech, so prosperity can come about only when the farmer and businessman enjoy economic freedom. The German leaders reduced tariffs, expanded free trade, lowered taxes. From 1950 to 1960 alone, the standard of living in West Germany and Berlin doubled.

Where four decades ago there was rubble, today in West Berlin there is the greatest industrial output of any city in Germany -- busy office blocks, fine homes and apartments, proud avenues, and the spreading lawns of parkland. Where a city's culture seemed to have been destroyed, today there are two great universities, orchestras and an opera, countless theaters, and museums. Where there was want, today there's abundance -- food, clothing, automobiles -- the wonderful goods of the Ku'damm. From devastation, from utter ruin, you Berliners have, in freedom, rebuilt a city that once again ranks as one of the greatest on Earth. The Soviets may have had other plans. But, my friends, there were a few things the Soviets didn't count on: Berliner herz, Berliner humor, ja, und Berliner schnauze. [Berliner heart, Berliner humor, yes, and a Berliner schnauze.] [Laughter]

In the 1950's, Khrushchev predicted: "We will bury you." But in the West today, we see a free world that has achieved a level of prosperity and well-being unprecedented in all human history. In the Communist world, we see failure, technological backwardness, declining standards of health, even want of the most basic kind -- too little food. Even today, the Soviet Union still cannot feed itself. After these four decades, then, there stands before the entire world one great and inescapable conclusion: Freedom leads to prosperity. Freedom replaces the ancient hatreds among the nations with comity and peace. Freedom is the victor.

And now the Soviets themselves may, in a limited way, be coming to understand the importance of freedom. We hear much from Moscow about a new policy of reform and openness. Some political prisoners have been released. Certain foreign news broadcasts are no longer being jammed. Some economic enterprises have been permitted to operate with greater freedom from state control. Are these the beginnings of profound changes in the Soviet state? Or are they token gestures, intended to raise false hopes in the West, or to strengthen the Soviet system without changing it? We welcome change and openness; for we believe that freedom and security go together, that the advance of human liberty can only strengthen the cause of world peace.

There is one sign the Soviets can make that would be unmistakable, that would advance dramatically the cause of freedom and peace. General Secretary Gorbachev, if you seek peace, if you seek prosperity for the Soviet Union and Eastern Europe, if you seek liberalization: Come here to this gate! Mr. Gorbachev, open this gate! Mr. Gorbachev, tear down this wall!

I understand the fear of war and the pain of division that afflict this continent -- and I pledge to you my country's efforts to help overcome these burdens. To be sure, we in the West must resist Soviet expansion. So we must maintain defenses of unassailable strength. Yet we seek peace; so we must strive to reduce arms on both sides. Beginning 10 years ago, the Soviets challenged the Western alliance with a grave new threat, hundreds of new and more deadly SS-20 nuclear missiles, capable of striking every capital in Europe. The Western alliance responded by committing itself to a counter-deployment unless the Soviets agreed to negotiate a better solution; namely, the elimination of such weapons on both sides. For many months, the Soviets refused to bargain in earnestness. As the alliance, in turn, prepared to go forward with its counter-deployment, there were difficult days -- days of protests like those during my 1982 visit to this city -- and the Soviets later walked away from the table.

But through it all, the alliance held firm. And I invite those who protested then -- I invite those who protest today -- to mark this fact: Because we remained strong, the Soviets came back to the table. And because we remained strong, today we have within reach the possibility, not merely of limiting the growth of arms, but of eliminating, for the first time, an entire class of nuclear weapons from the face of the Earth. As I speak, NATO ministers are meeting in Iceland to review the progress of our proposals for eliminating these weapons. At the talks in Geneva, we have also proposed deep cuts in strategic offensive weapons. And the Western allies have likewise made far-reaching proposals to reduce the danger of conventional war and to place a total ban on chemical weapons.

While we pursue these arms reductions, I pledge to you that we will maintain the capacity to deter Soviet aggression at any level at which it might occur. And in cooperation with many of our allies, the United States is pursuing the Strategic Defense Initiative research to base deterrence not on the threat of offensive retaliation, but on defenses that truly defend -- on systems, in short, that will not target populations, but shield them. By these means we seek to increase the safety of Europe and all the world. But we must remember a crucial fact: East and West do not mistrust each other because we are armed; we are armed because we mistrust each other. And our differences are not about weapons but about liberty. When President Kennedy spoke at the City Hall those 24 years ago, freedom was encircled, Berlin was under siege. And today, despite all the pressures upon this city, Berlin stands secure in its liberty. And freedom itself is transforming the globe.

In the Philippines, in South and Central America, democracy has been given a rebirth. Throughout the Pacific, free markets are working miracle after miracle of economic growth. In the industrialized nations a technological revolution is taking place -- a revolution marked by rapid, dramatic advances in computers and telecommunications.

In Europe, only one nation and those it controls refuse to join the community of freedom. Yet in this age of redoubled economic growth, of information and innovation, the Soviet Union faces a choice: It must make fundamental changes, or it will become obsolete. Today thus represents a moment of hope. We in the West stand ready to cooperate with the East to promote true openness, to break down barriers that separate people, to create a safer, freer world.

And surely there is no better place than Berlin, the meeting place of East and West, to make a start. Free people of Berlin: Today, as in the past, the United States stands for the strict observance and full implementation of all parts of the Four Power Agreement of 1971. Let us use this occasion, the 750th anniversary of this city, to usher in a new era, to seek a still fuller, richer life for the Berlin of the future. Together, let us maintain and develop the ties between the Federal Republic and the Western sectors of Berlin, which is permitted by the 1971 agreement. And I invite Mr. Gorbachev: Let us work to bring the Eastern and Western parts of the city closer together, so that all the inhabitants of all Berlin can enjoy the benefits that come with life in one of the great cities of the world. To open Berlin still further to all Europe, East and West, let us expand the vital air access to this city, finding ways of making commercial air service to Berlin more convenient, more comfortable, and more economical. We look to the day when West Berlin can become one of the chief aviation hubs in all central Europe.

With our French and British partners, the United States is prepared to help bring international meetings to Berlin. It would be only fitting for Berlin to serve as the site of United Nations meetings, or world conferences on human rights and arms control or other issues that call for international cooperation. There is no better way to establish hope for the future than to enlighten young minds, and we would be honored to sponsor summer youth exchanges, cultural events, and other programs for young Berliners from the East. Our French and British friends, I'm certain, will do the same. And it's my hope that an authority can be found in East Berlin to sponsor visits from young people of the Western sectors.

One final proposal, one close to my heart: Sport represents a source of enjoyment and ennoblement, and you may have noted that the Republic of Korea (South Korea) has offered to permit certain events of the 1988 Olympics to take place in the North. International sports competitions of all kinds could take place in both parts of this city. And what better way to demonstrate to the world the openness of this city than to offer in some future year to hold the Olympic games here in Berlin, East and West?

In these four decades, as I have said, you Berliners have built a great city. You've done so in spite of threats -- the Soviet attempts to impose the East-mark, the blockade. Today the city thrives in spite of the challenges implicit in the very presence of this wall. What keeps you here? Certainly there's a great deal to be said for your fortitude, for your defiant courage. But I believe there's something deeper, something that involves Berlin's whole look and feel and way of life -- not mere sentiment. No one could live long in Berlin without being completely disabused of illusions. Something instead, that has seen the difficulties of life in Berlin but chose to accept them, that continues to build this good and proud city in contrast to a surrounding totalitarian presence that refuses to release human energies or aspirations. Something that speaks with a powerful voice of affirmation, that says yes to this city, yes to the future, yes to freedom. In a word, I would submit that what keeps you in Berlin is love both profound and abiding.

Perhaps this gets to the root of the matter, to the most fundamental distinction of all between East and West. The totalitarian world produces backwardness because it does such violence to the spirit, thwarting the human impulse to create, to enjoy, to worship. The totalitarian world finds even symbols of love and of worship an affront. Years ago, before the East Germans began rebuilding their churches, they erected a secular structure: the television tower at Alexander Platz. Virtually ever since, the authorities have been working to correct what they view as the tower's one major flaw, treating the glass sphere at the top with paints and chemicals of every kind. Yet even today when the sun strikes that sphere -- that sphere that towers over all Berlin the light makes the sign of the cross. There in Berlin, like the city itself, symbols of love, symbols of worship, cannot be suppressed.

As I looked out a moment ago from the Reichstag, that embodiment of German unity, I noticed words crudely spray-painted upon the wall, perhaps by a young Berliner, "This wall will fall. Beliefs become reality." Yes, across Europe, this wall will fall. For it cannot withstand faith; it cannot withstand truth. The wall cannot withstand freedom.

And I would like, before I close, to say one word. I have read, and I have been questioned since I've been here about certain demonstrations against my coming. And I would like to say just one thing, and to those who demonstrate so. I wonder if they have ever asked themselves that if they should have the kind of government they apparently seek, no one would ever be able to do what they're doing again.

Thank you and God bless you all.

A Future that Works

1987

Thank you all. Thank you. As Henry VIII said to each one of his six wives, "I won't keep you long."

Fellow conservatives and dear friends, it's such a pleasure to be with you again. I see so many who've served our cause with such distinction over the years. David Keene and so many others of you deserve accolades for commitment and dedication.

What we've accomplished these last six years wouldn't have been possible without a solid foundation, one painstakingly laid. And much of that work was done by men and women who were content to make their contribution knowing their names would never be enshrined, individuals who didn't make the clips when the recent documentary about the conservative movement was made. Two centuries ago, the Americans who were the bulwark of the cause of liberty and independence -- [who] backed up the Hancocks, the Jeffersons, and the Patrick Henrys -- were of similar stock.

And so, today let me express my appreciation to all of you. You are truly freedom's team. The going may be a little rough at this moment, but let no one doubt our resolve. You know, these last several weeks, I've felt a little bit like that farmer that was driving his horse and wagon to town for some grain and had a head-on collision with a truck. And later was the litigation involving claims for his injuries, some of them permanent. And he was on the stand and a lawyer said to him, "Isn't it true that while you were lying there at the scene of the accident someone came over to you and asked you how you were feeling, and you said you never felt better in your life?" And he said, "Yes, I remember that."

Well, later he's on the stand and the witnesses were there -- the lawyer for the other side is questioning -- and he said, "When you gave that answer about how you felt, what were the circumstances?" "Well," he said, "I was lying there and a car came up and a deputy sheriff got out." He said, "My horse was screaming with pain -- had broken two legs. The deputy took out his gun, put it in the horse's ear, and finished him off." And he said, "My dog was whining with pain -- had a broken back. And," he said, "he went over to him and put the gun in his ear. And then," he says, "he turned to me and says now, how are you feeling?"

But getting back to our resolve: six years ago we won a great victory, and we don't intend to let anyone again drag our beloved country into the murky pit of collectivism and statism.

This is the 200th anniversary of our Constitution, and no cloud will dim the shining light of our remembrance. This year we rededicate ourselves to the shared values and the common purpose that have given our nation unrivaled prosperity and freedom. We hear the cynics, but pay them no mind. We pass by the pessimists and the doomsayers, knowing that they'll always be with us, but confident that they no longer can hold our country back unless we let them. We see before us a future worthy of our past and a tomorrow greater than all our yesterdays. If there's any message that I wish to convey today, it is: be of good cheer. We're coming back and coming back strong.

Our confidence flows not from our skill at maneuvering through political mazes, not from our ability to make the right deal at the right time, nor from any idea of playing one interest group off against the other. Unlike our opponents, who find their glee in momentary political leverage, we [nourish] our strength of purpose from a commitment to ideals that we deeply believe are not only right but that work.

Ludwig Von Mises, that great economist, once noted: "People must fight for something they want to achieve, not simply reject an evil." Well, the conservative movement remains in the ascendancy because we have a bold, forward-looking agenda. No longer can it be said that conservatives are just anti-Communist. We are, and proudly so, but we are also the keepers of the flame of liberty. And as such, we believe that America should be a source of support, both moral and material, for all those on God's Earth who struggle for freedom. Our cause is their cause, whether it be in Nicaragua, Afghanistan, or Angola. When I came back from Iceland I said -- and I meant it -- American foreign policy is not simply focused on the prevention of war but the expansion of freedom. Modern conservatism is an active, not a reactive philosophy.

It's not just in opposition to those vices that debase character and community, but affirms values that are at the heart of civilization. We favor protecting and strengthening the family, an institution that was taken for granted during the decades of liberal domination of American government.

The family, as became clear in the not-too-distant past, is taken for granted at our peril. Victimized most were the least fortunate among us, those who sorely needed the strength and protection of the family. A federal welfare system, constructed in the name of helping those in poverty, wreaked havoc on the poor family --

tearing it apart, eating away at the underpinnings of their community, creating fatherless children, and unprecedented despair. The liberal welfare state has been a tragedy beyond description for so many of our fellow citizens, a crime against less fortunate Americans. The welfare system cries out for reform, and reformed it will be. And when it is, the No. I question that must be asked of every change is: will this strengthen the family?

Now, personally, I think that criterion should guide our decisions, not just in welfare reform, but in the deliberations of every department and agency. And if the answer is negative, the proposal should be sent to the Heritage Foundation for study, and you can bet they'll know what to do with it.

Our positive stance on family and children is consistent with our heartfelt convictions on the issue of abortion. Here again, we're not just against an evil. We're not just anti-abortion; we're pro-life. Many who consider abortion the taking of human life understandably feel frustrated and perhaps a sense of helplessness in bringing about the legal changes that we all seek. Progress has been slow and painful, and all the while the taking of unborn lives continues. Well, while we keep up the pressure for a change of law, there is something that can be done. Those of us who oppose abortion can and should aggressively move forward with a positive adoption versus abortion campaign.

We must see to it that adoption is a readily available alternative and is an encouraged course of action. I would like to commend those in our movement, while not easing up on applying political pressure, who have been involved in providing counseling and services, especially to unwed mothers. Every time a choice is made to save an unborn baby's life, it is reason for joy. In the meantime, we in government will see to it that not one tax dollar goes to encouraging any woman to snuff out the life of her unborn child and that eventually the life of the unborn again comes within the protection of the law.

Last week we sent to Congress legislation to enact on a permanent, government-wide basis the Hyde amendment restriction on federal funding of abortion. Our proposal would also cut off funding, under Title X, to private organizations that refer or perform abortions except when the mother's life is in danger. I hope all of you will join in the bipartisan effort to enact this much needed legislation.

Conservatives are working for a society where children are cherished and in school are taught not only reading, writing, and arithmetic but fundamental values as well. And in striving for this, we will not compromise in our commitment to restore the right to pray to the school children of America. We want a strong America, and we know the truth behind President Eisenhower's words, when he quoted a young Frenchman's observation that if America ceases to be good, America will cease to be great.

The moral underpinnings of our country must be able to bear the weight of today if we're to pass on to the next generation an America worth having. And again, we're positive, and our eyes are on the future. And that's why so many of today's young people are supporting our cause. And believe me, as I was running for re-election, I saw them at every stop -- those young people full of life, enjoying their freedom, and enthusiastic about the United States of America. I have to tell you, you young people are a new experience for us. We went through some years when you weren't cheering us, and it's wonderful to have you on our side. Well, our greatest political challenge is to find the formula that will mobilize our broad support among young people. Clearly, they aren't just looking for youthful appearances. My birthday cake's beginning to look more and more like a bonfire every year!

We must offer a vision of a future that works, a positive agenda for positive results. And we must not be so much against big government and high taxes as we are in favor of higher take-home pay and more freedom. And we've proven it works. With an emphasis on enterprise, investment, and work, on jobs and opportunity, we turned around economic decline and national malaise and set in motion one of the longest periods of peacetime economic growth and job creation in postwar history.

The pundits, you know, the pundits told us that we couldn't expect to get anything accomplished, even before we got to Washington. Now, they're trying to bring the curtain down before the show is over. Well, I learned a lesson in my former profession. So, let me give you a tip: we're saving the best stuff for the last act. Thank you. Thank you very much. Thank you.

Thank you very much. Our game plan is still the best one in town. The notion that government controls, central planning, and bureaucracy can provide cost-free prosperity has now come and gone the way of the hula-hoop, the Nehru jackets, and the all-asparagus diet. Throughout the world the failure of socialism is evident.

There's air underground joke that's told in the Soviet Union, for example, about a teacher who asked one of the young students, Ivan, what life is like in the United States. And dutifully Ivan said,

"Half the people are unemployed and millions are hungry or starving." "Well, then," the teacher asks, "then what is the goal of the Soviet Union?" Ivan said, "To catch up with the United States."

Seriously, though, today free enterprise is propelling us into a new technological era. Small businesses throughout our land now have computer capability, which a decade ago was available only to large corporations. The economic vitality pushing our country into the 21st Century is broad-based and irreversible -- and it's not coming from the top, but from the bottom. The creative talents of our citizenry, always America's greatest asset, are being magnified by state-of-the-art technology and put to work for our benefit as never before. We have every reason to be optimistic.

Our scientific advances offer us new methods of meeting the challenges we face as a people. One of the first significant questions to emerge as a result of our rapid progress deals with the Strategic Defense Initiative. I see you know that that is our effort to develop a way of protecting mankind from the threat of ballistic missiles. It holds the promise of someday making those missiles, deadly weapons that have been the cause of such dread, obsolete.

We have offered to share the benefits of our SDI program with the Soviet Union, perhaps as part of an overall agreement to dramatically reduce our respective nuclear arsenals. But let me make this clear: a defense against ballistic missiles is just one of many new achievements that will be made possible by the incredible technological progress that we are enjoying.

Each step forward improves our lives, adding to our ability to produce and build and generate wealth. Yet each step also has strategic implications. SDI, as I say, is one. Let there be no doubt, we have no intention of being held back because our adversary cannot keep up. We will use our scientific skills to make this a more prosperous world and to enhance the security of our own country. We must not and will not bargain our future away.

Six years ago we came to Washington at a time of great national uncertainty. The vigor and confidence so evident in our land today reflect more than luck. They are the outgrowth of ideas that stress freedom for the individual and respect for the humane and decent values of family, God and neighborhood.

We are giving our children the greatest gift that is within our power to give, the one we received from those who came before us: a strong, free, and opportunity-filled America. And I thank you for all that you have done and continue to do to make certain that we do just that.

And so, thank you, and God bless you all.

On The Frontier of Freedom

February 11, 1988

Thank you very much. It's great to be here tonight, and I'm delighted to see so many old friends. And now let's get right to it. First, there's the INF treaty. How do you think I felt when Gorbachev called a week and a half ago and asked me if our first group of on-site inspectors could be the Denver Broncos' pass defense? (Laughter.) And then along came the House vote on Contra aid -- I felt so terrible, I nearly called Dan Reeves and John Elway to tell them what a rough week I'd had.

But seriously, while the Denver Broncos are all terrific athletes and people, each one of us has to congratulate the Washington Redskins. Believe me, the House action on the Contra vote was a missed chance at a victory for peace in Central America. It's great to know there are some people in Washington who play to win. And believe me, I'll be getting back to that topic in a few minutes.

By the way, something odd happened just before I got here tonight that I think you should know about. I got a message from Dave Keene reminding me that this was the eve of Lincoln's birthday -- and suggesting I go upstairs and check on the ghost in Lincoln's bedroom. I did. And what do you know, there was Stan Evans dressed as Abe Lincoln. And he kept saying, "Listen to Jesse Helms."

Actually, I do want to thank you for that warm welcome, but I hope tonight isn't going to be like what happened to that fellow I knew back in Hollywood in those movie days -- and, oh, how I hope I haven't told you this one before.

We had an actor that was in Hollywood, and he was only there long enough to get enough money to go to Italy, because he aspired to an operatic career. And then after some time there, in Milan, Italy, where he was studying, he was invited to sing at La Scala, the very spiritual fountainhead of opera. They were doing Pagliacci, and he sang the beautiful aria, Vesti La Giuba. And he received such thunderous and sustained applause from the balconies and the orchestra seats that he had to repeat the aria as an encore. And again the same sustained, thunderous applause. And again he sang Vesti La Giuba. And this went on until finally he motioned for quiet, and he tried to tell them how full his heart was at that reception -- his first time out. But he said, "I have sung Vesti La Giuba nine times now. My voice is gone. I cannot do it again." And a voice from the balcony said, "You'll do it till you get it right." Well, let's get it right tonight. And let's start where we should start.

A couple of weeks ago, I talked about the state of our Union, and tonight I'd like to talk about something that I think in many ways is synonymous: the state of our movement. During the past year, plenty of questions have been asked about the conservative movement by some people who were surprised to find out back in 1980 that there was such a thing. I mean a powerful new political movement capable of running a victorious national campaign based on an unabashed appeal to the American people for conservative ideas and principles.

Well, we conservatives have been in Washington now for a while and we occasionally need to remind ourselves what brought us here in the first place: our unshakable, root-deep, all-encompassing skepticism about the capital city's answer to the UFO, that bizarre, ever-tottering but ever-flickering saucer in the sky called "The Prevailing Washington Wisdom."

And, right now, some of the Potomac seers are saying we conservatives are tired; or they're saying we don't have a candidate, some of those candidates in the other party saying how easy it's going to be to win the presidency for their liberal agenda because they can run on, of all things, this administration's economic record. Boy, have I got news for them. They're seeing flying saucers again. I've even got a quote for them. It's from Napoleon -- the morning of Waterloo -- at breakfast with his generals. This is true. He said, "I tell you what -- Wellington is a bad general. The English are bad troops. We'll settle the matter by lunchtime."

Well, my fellow conservatives, I think that's exactly what this year is about -- settling the matter by lunchtime. Letting the liberals in Washington discover once again the lesson they refuse to learn. Letting them know just how big our election year will be because of booming economic growth and individual opportunity; and how big an election year ball and chain they've given themselves with a seven-year record of opposition to the real record. But, most of all, letting them know that the real friends of the conservative movement aren't those entrenched in the capital city for 50 years; the real friends of the conservative movement are an entity that gets heard from in a big way every four years and who, I promise you, are going to be heard from this year. I'm talking about those who, if the case is aggressively put before them, will vote for limited government, family values, and a tough, strong foreign policy every single time. I'm talking about those believers in common sense and sound values, your friends and mine, the American people.

You see, those who underestimate the conservative movement are the same people who always underestimate the American people. Take the latest instance. As I mentioned, in recent months some people -- and I'm not mentioning any names because I don't want to build up any candidacies before New Hampshire, but you know who they are -- have actually taken it upon themselves to prove to the American people that they've been worse off under this administration than they were back in the Carter years of the '70s.

Now I agree with you, this takes some doing. How do they manage it? Well, you see, any statistical comparison of the two recent administrations would start with 1977 to 1981 as the budget years of the last administration, and 1981 to 1987 as the pertinent years for this one. Now, that sounds reasonable enough. But our opponents have a new approach, one that would have embarrassed even the emperor's tailors. They take the years 1977, to up to 1983 -- and then they stop. So you see, not only do 1984 and 1985 not get counted in their data base, but they include in this administration's economic record four years of the last Democratic administration. As columnist Warren Brookes pointed out in an article published in the Washington Times, "all of the foreshortened Reagan gains are nullified by the Carter losses, so they look like no gains at all, or, worse, losses." Our successes, in short, are buried under the last administration's failures.

But the truth is otherwise. Because under the last administration real per capita disposable income rose at only one percent annual rate, only half the two percent rate of increase under this administration's gain that has totaled 12.4 percent in six years. Under the last administration, median family income declined 6.8 percent, while under this administration it went up 9.1 percent. Or take the real after-tax labor income per hour: If you use the approach adopted by our liberal critics, you see a 4.5 percent decline. But the truth is that that figure fell 8.5 percent under the last administration and we turned this around and accounted for an 8.9 percent increase.

Under the last administration, the average weekly wage went down an incredible 10 percent in real terms, which accounted for the worst drop in postwar history. Here again, we've stopped the decline. And that's not to mention what all this has meant in terms of opportunity for women, for blacks, and minorities, the very groups our opponents say they most want to help.

Well, since the recovery began, 70 percent of the new jobs have been translated into opportunities for women; and black and other minority employment has risen twice as fast as all other groups. Minority family income has also increased at a rate over 40 percent faster than other groups. In addition, since 1983, 2.9 million people have climbed out of poverty, and the poverty rate has declined at the fastest rate in more than 10 years.

So, think for a moment on what these statistics mean and the kind of political nerve and desperation it takes to try to sell the American people on the idea that in the 1980s they never had it so bad. The truth is, we're in the 63rd month of this non-stop expansion. Real Gross National Product growth for 1987 was 3.8 percent, defying the pessimists and even exceeding our own forecast -- which was criticized as being too rosy at the time -- by more than one half percent. Inflation is down from 13.5 per cent in 1980 to only around 4 percent or less this year. And there's over 15 million new jobs.

So, believe me, I welcome this approach by the opposition. And I promise you, every time they use it, I'll just tell the story of a friend of mine who was asked to a costume ball a short time ago -- he slapped some egg on his face and went as a liberal economist. Now the reason I spell out these statistics and stress this economic issue should be very clear. You know that some cynics like to say that the people vote their pocketbook. But that's not quite the point. Economic issues are important to the people not simply for reasons of self-interest. They know the whole body politic depends on economic stability; the great crises have come for democracies when taxes and inflation ran out of control and undermined social relations and basic institutions. The American people know what limited government, tax cuts, deregulation, and the move towards privatization have meant. It's meant the largest peacetime expansion in our history, and I can guarantee you they won't want to throw that away for a return to budgets beholden to the liberal special interests.

No, I think the economic record of conservatives in power is going to speak for itself. But now let's turn to another area. For two decades we've been talking about getting justices on the Supreme Court who cared less about criminals and more about the victims of crime, justices who knew that the words "original intent" referred to something more than New Year's resolutions and fad diets. And then, seven months ago a seat opened on the Supreme Court. And even before our first nominee was announced, a campaign was planned unlike any that has ever been waged for or against a judicial nominee in the history of our country. And let me acknowledge once again my admiration for one of the courageous defenders, not only in our time but in all time, of the principles of our Constitution, yes, of its original intent -- Judge Robert Bork.

One of America's most cherished principles -- the independence and integrity of our judiciary -- was under siege. And the American people, who have always been with the ultimate guarantors of the Constitution, began to say with clarity and finality, it must never happen again. So when I nominated a judge who could as easily have been my first nominee, there was hardly a peep of protest. And Judge Kennedy is now going to be Justice Kennedy. And since our opponents won't, I'll let you in on a secret -- Judge Kennedy will be just the kind of justice that you and I've been determined to put on the Court, Anyway, any man who teaches law school in a tri-corner hat and a powdered wig is okay by me on original intent.

Let's look at how far and how successfully we've carried the battle into the lower courts. Just look at the statistics on criminal sentencing. In few places can you see more clearly the collapse of the liberal stranglehold on our courts. The most recent statistics show federal judges imposed prison sentences that averaged 32 percent longer than those handed down during 1979. Robbery sentences were 10 percent longer; drug offenses, 38 percent longer; and weapons offenses, 41 percent longer.

The great legal debates of the past two decades over criminal justice have, at their root, been debates over a strict versus expansive construction of the Constitution. The Constitution, as originally intended by the framers, is itself tough on crime, and protective of the victims of crime. For so long the liberal message to our national culture was tune in, turn on, let it all hang out. And now they see conservatives taking the lead as our nation says "no" to drugs, and "yes" to family, and "absolutely" to schools that teach basic skills, basic values, and basic discipline. And it's no wonder that our nation admires a man who believes in teaching values in education, and talks turkey to teachers, parents, and educators, such as our Secretary of Education, Bill Bennett.

And so I say to you tonight that the vision and record that we will take aggressively to the American people this November is a vision that all Americans, except a few on the left, share. A vision of a nation that believes in the heroism of ordinary people living ordinary lives; of tough courts and safe streets, of a drug-free America where schools teach honesty, respect, love of learning and, yes, love of country; a vision of a land where families can grow in love and safety and where dreams are made with opportunity. This is the vision; this is the record; this is the agenda for victory this year. Well, that's the record then on the economy and the social issues. Now, let's turn to foreign policy.

I want to be clear tonight about the vote on Contra aid. It was a setback to the national security interests of the United States, and a sad moment for the cause of peace and freedom in Central America. Until now the carrot-and-stick approach has worked in forcing a Communist regime to relax some of its repression. But now, the action by the House of Representatives removes one part of that formula and goes only with the carrot. The effect of this vote then was to trust the promises of democracy of the Sandinista Communists -- the kind of promises that no Communist regime in history has ever carried out, and that this regime was likely to carry out only under continued pressure. The effect of this vote was to rest the hopes for peace and democracy in Central America purely and simply on the word of the Communist regime in Managua. This course is, and I repeat, a risk to America's national security.

But you know, I read something the other day and it's worth a note here. One of those opposing aid to the freedom fighters said it was important to get a 20-vote margin. Well, as you know, it was nothing like that -- if we could have turned around four or five votes, we would have won. Last week's vote was not the final word, only a pause. Last week, the bad news was the lost vote in the House. But the good news was our support in the Senate and the overwhelming number of House Republicans who voted with us and those 47 Democrats who braved the threats of reprisals to vote for Contra aid.

So, let me make this pledge to you tonight: we're not giving up on those who are fighting for their freedom -- and they aren't giving up either. I'll have more to say on this in a few weeks. For now, I'll leave it at this: get ready -- the curtain hasn't fallen, the drama continues.

While we're on foreign policy, let me turn for just a moment to what I said in that December interview while Mr. Gorbachev was here. You know, Ben Wattenberg was one of the journalists there, and he brought up a speech I made back in 1982 to the British Parliament. And he asked me if what I really was saying was what I said in England: that if the West remained resolute, the Soviets would have to, at some point, deal with their own internal problems and crises, that the tides of history are shifting in favor of the cause of freedom. Well, I believed then, and I believe now, that we must consider what we're seeing -- or the steps in that direction. This hardly means accepting the Soviets at face value. Few of us can forget what that has led to in the past. FDR was quoted as saying during his dealings with Stalin -- with the Soviets in '44: "Stalin doesn't want anything but security for his country and I think that if

I give him everything I possibly can and ask nothing from him in return, noblesse oblige, he won't try to annex anything and will work with me for a world democracy and peace."

Well, no, there is no room for illusion. Our guard is up, our watch is careful. We shall not be led by -- or misled by -- atmospherics. We came to Washington with a common-sense message that the world is a dangerous place where the only sure route to peace and the protection of freedom is through American strength. In no place has this thesis of peace through strength been tested more than on the matter of intermediate-range nuclear forces (INF). In deploying over 400 SS-20s, with over 1,200 warheads, against our friends and allies in Europe and Asia over the past decade, the Soviets were playing a high-stakes game of geopolitical blackjack. The prize was Europe -- the strategy, discredit America's deterrence and undermine the NATO alliance. But we and our allies turned over a winning hand, deploying in Europe Pershing II and ground-launched cruise missiles that provided an effective counter to the new Soviet missiles, and Moscow finally stopped upping the stakes.

What I would like to see is for some of those who've been praising our INF treaty to show they've learned its true lesson and vote to maintain an adequate defense budget, our work on a strategic defense against ballistic missiles, and, yes, aid to the freedom fighters in Nicaragua.

And while we're on the subject of our nation's defense -- you know, there's a man I want to talk about tonight who said once that "the definition of happiness was service to a noble cause." No one has done that better, and tonight I salute Cap Weinberger for all he's done for America.

But at the same time we must not look at any single step alone -- we must see not just the INF treaty but also the advance of SDI and, most important, the growing democratic revolution around the globe against totalitarian regimes. We should engage the Soviets in negotiations to deter war and keep the peace. But at the same time, we must make clear our own position, as I have throughout these negotiations. In sitting down to these negotiations, we accept no moral equivalency between the cause of freedom and the rule of totalitarianism.

And we understand that the most important change of all is this: that containment is no longer enough, that we no longer can be satisfied with an endless stalemate between liberty and repression. That arms reduction negotiations, development and testing of SDI, and our help for freedom fighters around the globe must express the clear goal of American foreign policy. To deter war, yes. To further world peace, yes. But, most of all, to advance and protect the cause of world freedom so that some day every man, woman, and child on this Earth has as a birthright the full blessings of liberty.

We've seen dramatic change in these seven years. Who would have guessed seven years ago that we would see tax rates drop from 70 percent to 28 percent, the longest peacetime economic boom in our history, or a massive shift in world opinion toward the ideas of free enterprise and political freedom?

I know some of you are impatient with the pace of this change. But if I might repeat a story I told when I addressed you for the first time as President -- I had the pleasure in appearing before a Senate committee once while I was still Governor. And I was challenged there because there was a Republican president in the White House at the time, who'd been there for some time and why hadn't we corrected everything that had gone wrong. And the only way I could think to answer him is, I told him about a ranch many years ago that Nancy and I acquired. It had a barn with eight stalls in it, in which they kept cattle-cows. We wanted to keep horses. Well, the accumulation within the stalls had built up the floor to the place that it wasn't even tall enough for horses in there. And so there I was, day after day, with a pick and shovel, lowering the level of those stalls, which had accumulated over the years. And I told this Senator who'd asked that question that I discovered that you didn't undo in a relatively short time what it had taken some 15 years to accumulate.

We have not only been undoing the damage of the past; we've put this nation on the upward road again. And, in the process, the differences between the liberals and conservatives have become clear to the American people. We want to keep taxes low, they want to raise them; we send in budgets with spending cuts and they want to ignore them; we want the balanced budget amendment and the line-item veto and they oppose them; we want tough judges and tough anti-crime legislation, they hold them both up in the Congress.

You'd be surprised how many judges are waiting out there before they -- so that they have to pass on them before they can take their office, and they've been waiting for months. We want a prayer amendment, they won't let it come to a vote in the House; we stress firmness with the Soviets, they try to pass legislation that would tie our hands in arms negotiations and endanger our defenses. But I say, we have a program and a plan for the American people -- a program to protect American jobs by fighting the menace of protectionism, to move forward at flank speed with SDI, to call America to conscience on the issue of abortion on demand, to mention, as I did in my State of the Union Address, the overwhelming importance of family life and family values.

That's a case to take to the American people. That's a fighting agenda. I intend to campaign vigorously for whoever our nominee is, and tonight I ask each of you to join me in this important crusade. Let's ask the American people to replenish our mandate. Let's tell them if they want four more years of economic progress and the march of world freedom, they must help us this year. Help us settle the matter before lunchtime. Help make 1988 the year of the Waterloo liberal.

I just have to add here, when you look at the figures overall -- that they have the nerve even to still be out there and campaigning. (Laughter)

We mustn't just think that electing the president is enough. We've been doing that for more than half-a-century. We have -- in the 50 years between 1931 and 1980, only four years in that period was there a Republican majority in both houses of the Congress -- two years in Eisenhower's regime, two years in Truman's. But for 46 of those 50 years, they controlled the Congress. Every Democratic president, except for those two years, had a Democratic Congress. Every Republican president had a Democratic Congress, except for those two years in Eisenhower's regime. And now, in the last seven years added to that -- yes, for six of those years we had one House. But except for the four years, for 58 years it will be our opponents holding the House of Representatives, where so much legislation and authorization for spending and so forth comes in. And in all those 58 years, there have only been eight single years in which there was a balanced budget. So, who's at fault for the deficit today?

Back when the great society -- when the war on poverty began, which poverty won -- from 1965 to 1980 -- in those 15 years, the federal budget increased to five times what it had been in '65. And the deficit increased to 38 times what it had been just 15 years before. It's built-in, it's structural. And you and I need to get representatives not only in the Executive Branch, but out there in the legislature, so that we can change that structure that is so built-in, and that threatens us with so much harm.

Well, I've gone on too long for all of you here, but I just wanted to -- I couldn't resist, because you're the troops. You're out there on the frontier of freedom. One young soldier over there in Korea -- one of our men -- saluted me when I visited there, and very proudly said, "Mr. President, we're on the frontier of freedom." Well, so are you.

Thank you. God bless you all.

Announcement of Alzheimer's Disease

November 5, 1994

My fellow Americans, I have recently been told that I am one of the millions of Americans who will be afflicted with Alzheimer's disease.

Upon learning this news, Nancy and I had to decide whether as private citizens we would keep this a private matter or whether we would make this news known in a public way. In the past, Nancy suffered from breast cancer and I had my cancer surgeries. We found through our open disclosures we were able to raise public awareness. We were happy that as a result, many more people underwent testing. They were treated in early stages and able to return to normal, healthy lives.

So now we feel it is important to share it with you. In opening our hearts, we hope this might promote greater awareness of this condition. Perhaps it will encourage a clearer understanding of the individuals and families who are affected by it.

At the moment I feel just fine. I intend to live the remainder of the years God gives me on this Earth doing the things I have always done. I will continue to share life's journey with my beloved Nancy and my family. I plan to enjoy the great outdoors and stay in touch with my friends and supporters.

Unfortunately, as Alzheimer's disease progresses, the family often bears a heavy burden. I only wish there was some way I could spare Nancy from this painful experience. When the time comes, I am confident that with your help she will face it with faith and courage.

In closing, let me thank you, the American people, for giving me the great honor of allowing me to serve as your president. When the Lord calls me home, whenever that day may be, I will leave with the greatest love for this country of ours and eternal optimism for its future.

I now begin the journey that will lead me into the sunset of my life. I know that for America there will always be a bright dawn ahead.

Thank you, my friends. May God always bless you.

Statements following the
Death of President Reagan

June 5, 2004

Public email and attachments of a Georgia State Senator

Dear Friends in the Third Senate District,

I wanted to share the following press release with you from the Governor's Office regarding President Ronald Reagan. Below the Governor's press statement is a tribute from Pastor Don Cole, who is the Republican Chairman of Doughtery County and who also serves on the State Board of the Department of Human Resources. I have also included an email sent out by Attorney and Judge, Hal Moroz, of Camden County, who has issued a challenge to all of us.

Most of us can say we've been inspired by Ronald Reagan, and perhaps that is even why many of us are involved in Republican political efforts today. As Republicans and as Americans, we have principles worth defending, and President Reagan knew exactly what they were and never retreated. He challenged all of us to be proud to be Americans and to be the best we could be, to be that shining city set upon a hill. We have lost some of our bearings since the days of President Reagan, but it is my hope we will regain our moral character as a nation and do all we can to pass a brighter torch to the next generation.

With hope for the future,
Jeff Chapman
State Senate, Brunswick, Georgia

Statement of Governor Perdue Regarding the Passing of President Ronald Reagan

ATLANTA, GA - Governor Sonny Perdue issued the following statement today regarding the passing of President Ronald Reagan:

"Mary and I join the American people in mourning the passing of President Reagan. At a time when our nation was struggling to find its sense of purpose, President Reagan's optimism and commitment to our founding principles restored faith in our country and renewed America's enduring spirit. He boldly advanced the cause of freedom to every corner of the world, leading to the end of the Cold War, and his confidence in our nation's economy led to one of the strongest periods of economic growth in U.S. history.

"Our nation has known many great leaders, and President Reagan will be remembered in history as one of the greatest. He made each one of us proud to be an American. He instilled in all of us the belief that everyone can achieve the American Dream.

"In the twilight of his life, as she had done for half a century, his beloved Nancy stood by her husband. Today, we extend our condolences to her and the entire Reagan family. May God continue to bless the nation that President Reagan so deeply loved and honorably served, and may we always strive to be that shining city upon a hill."

Governor Perdue signed an executive order today ordering all state flags lowered to half staff for a period of mourning of 30 days consistent with federal law.

President Ronald Reagan Leaves a Legacy

He will go down in history as one of the greatest Presidents of our great nation. He took office at a time when America desperately sought for positive, optimistic, strong leadership. He provided the leadership and America rose to the expectations that he knew that she could. On the day of his inauguration, the Iranian government released Americans who had been held hostage ending a crisis that had paralyzed our nation for 444 days. It was no accident that the crisis swiftly ended when he came to office. The Iranians knew that Ronald Reagan was a man of principle and strength and that he would act decisively if they didn't. His principled strength set America back on the course of being the "shining city on a hill."

Ronald Reagan didn't bring about sweeping change by himself. Sweeping change came about because he took the obstacles out of the way for Americans to believe in themselves again. He led the way to slash taxes which brought about the greatest economic recovery our nation has experienced. He boldly challenged the Soviet Union, calling it an "evil empire." Liberals reacted in fear and trembling. So did the Soviet Union. Ronald Regan demanded, "Mr. Gorbachev, tear down this wall!" Ronald Reagan lived to see the evil empire fall and the opportunity for freedom arise.

The phrase "Reagan Revolution" characterizes the sweeping changes that our nation experienced starting with his eight years in office. We bought our first house in November of 1980. The interest rate was 13% and climbing when we closed on our home loan. Today the interest rates on mortgages are around 4%. Unemployment dropped, tax rates dropped, yet tax revenues went up because of the economic engine that cranked up when Reagan pushed for massive tax cuts. Our nation's defense structure and morale of our armed forces had been decimated after the lack of resolve to win in Vietnam. Ronald Reagan built it back and refused to take second place to anyone in the world. Our nation experienced a sense of pride and patriotism because President Ronald Reagan was not ashamed to express pride, patriotism, and a sense of national destiny. He was humble and held the office of President in reverence and respect. He would not enter the Oval Office without a coat and tie because the office deserved that kind of respect. Americans just needed a leader who expressed the feelings of the average American and Ronald Reagan was the man who finally said that, once again, it was ok to be proud to be an American.

Our world is a better place because God placed Ronald Reagan in our path. His legacy lives on today. We have a President who expresses the same patriotic, positive, principled resolve to lead and be a beacon of light to a world of darkness. Thank you, Ronald Reagan for leading the way and reminding America of how great, how blessed, and what a responsibility we carry in this world.

From the Desk of Judge Hal Moroz

Since the sad news of President Reagan's death, many friends, old and new, have contacted me on just how one might pay tribute to the memory of our beloved 40th President.

Well, I would strongly encourage everyone who might read this message and desire to do something to honor the life and works of President Reagan to join the Ronald Reagan Presidential Foundation. I have been a member for many years. At this time, the Foundation is also accepting messages of sympathy to First Lady Nancy Reagan. This can be done online at http://www.ronaldreaganmemorial.com or by writing THE RONALD REAGAN PRESIDENTIAL FOUNDATION, 40 Presidential Drive, Simi Valley, California 93065

I offered my condolences to Mrs. Reagan ... and here is what I wrote:

Dear Mrs. Reagan,

You have the profound condolences of me, my family, and a grateful Nation ... a nation that your husband made great again!

Your husband had a great influence on my life, and was a man I looked up to as a father figure years after my father died in 1963, just a month before President Kennedy's assassination. I thank God for having given me the opportunity to meet your husband, to embrace him, and to share his vision of America. To meet someone is one thing, but to spend time with someone is to have them become a part of your life ... you and President Reagan are a treasured and very special part of my life.

When he lost his bid for the Presidential nomination in 1976 to Gerald Ford, and Jimmy Carter was elected, I was devastated ...

... but even in losing, your husband taught me about dignity and grace, and to never give up, always be loyal, and keep faith in God and His hand on America's future ... he was the ultimate champion of the good that is America!

Whatever success I have achieved in life, whether as a husband, father, judge, whatever I am called to be, I owe in great part to your husband. In my many years of service as an Army Infantry officer, I said this to the wives and families of soldiers I commanded and had the great privilege of leading, but who unfortunately died in the line of duty: "We can take consolation in the promise of God ... His Word tells us that to be absent from the body is to be present with the Lord." I believe this is true for all believers, particularly of your husband.

On this day, your husband, my President, is surely in the presence of God, close enough to reach out and touch His face.

I mourn for our America without President Reagan, and I thank God for having giving us a brief shining moment with one of His most noble servants. Your husband now truly does belong to the Ages, and I shall miss him.

God bless you, my lady, and thank you on behalf of this very grateful American.

Very respectfully, I remain,

At your service,

Hal Moroz

~ * ~

This is the Age of Reagan! Let's Resurrect his memory, and ...

"Let's Make America Great Again!"

About the Author

Judge Hal Moroz

Hal Moroz is an Attorney and Counselor at Law, who has served as a county judge and city chief judge in the State of Georgia. Judge Moroz has represented individual clients and small, medium and large businesses in a variety of legal matters. And his practice in the law has ranged from small claims courts to the Supreme Court of the United States.

Judge Moroz is a retired U.S. Army officer, having served in the Airborne Infantry. He was first commissioned a Second Lieutenant in July of 1981 at Fort Bragg, N.C., the "Home of the 82d Airborne Division," by President Reagan's Secretary of the Army, the Hon. John O. Marsh, Jr.

Judge Moroz has served on the faculty of Florida Coastal School of Law in Jacksonville, Florida, and the State Bar of Georgia's Institute for Continuing Legal Education (ICLE). He is a former candidate for the U.S. Congress, and served as Special Counsel to the Georgia Republican Party's First Congressional District Committee in the 2000 primary and general elections, and went on to serve as a Presidential Ballot Inspector/Observer during the 2000 "recount" in Florida. Following the 2000 election, Judge Moroz was a candidate for federal judgeships in the U.S. District Court for the Middle District of Florida and the U.S. District Court for the Northern District of Illinois.

Judge Moroz is the founder of the Veterans Law Center, Inc., a non-profit, 501(c)(3) charitable organization that serves the interests of

America's 24 million military veterans   Located on the internet at VeteransLawCenter.org, the Veterans Law Center provides support and counsel to America's honorably discharged veterans, wherever they may be, and they do this free of charge to them.

Hal Moroz is also a prolific writer, having authored numerous legal articles, weekly legal newspaper columns, and books. Copies of his many books can be ordered at Amazon.com or any major online bookstore!

Hal Moroz can be reached through an internet search
or through his email at: hal@morozlaw.com or his website: MorozLaw.com

~ * ~

"A wise man will hear, and will increase learning; and a man of understanding shall attain unto wise counsels: To understand a proverb, and the interpretation; the words of the wise, and their dark sayings."

~ Proverbs 1:5-6

~ * ~

Judge Moroz Supports the Veterans Law Center!

If you would like to Support the VLC,
please read the following page ...

Want to support the Veterans Law Center in its charitable work?

Make a tax-deductible contribution to the Veterans Law Center by

(1) Going online to the **VeteransLawCenter.org**
& clicking **"Donate"**

~ and ~

**(2) Whenever you shop online at Amazon, please go to
AmazonSmile [https://smile.amazon.com] , name the "Veterans
Law Center" as your charity of choice,
and place your order**, and Amazon will make a contribution to the
Veterans Law Center.
It costs you nothing, and Amazon makes the donation!

EIN: 26-1822334

FLORIDA REGISTRATION #: CH29264
A COPY OF THE OFFICIAL REGISTRATION AND FINANCIAL INFORMATION MAY BE OBTAINED FROM THE
DIVISION OF CONSUMER SERVICES BY CALLING TOLL-FREE (800-435-7352) WITHIN THE STATE.
REGISTRATION DOES NOT IMPLY ENDORSEMENT, APPROVAL, OR RECOMMENDATION BY THE STATE.

www.ingramcontent.com/pod-product-compliance
Lightning Source LLC
Chambersburg PA
CBHW060238290526
45789CB00001B/94